RELIGION, FEMINISM, *and* FREEDOM *of* CONSCIENCE

*There is one thing stronger than all the armies
in the world, and that is an idea whose time has come.*
—Victor Hugo

Religion, Feminism, *and* Freedom *of* Conscience

A MORMON/HUMANIST DIALOGUE

EDITED BY GEORGE D. SMITH

Prometheus Books
Buffalo

Signature Books
Salt Lake City

1994

Cover design by Julie Easton.

Cover illustration by Carol Norby.

∞ *Religion, Feminism, and Freedom of Conscience* was printed on acid-free paper meeting the permanence of paper requirements of the American National Standard for Information Sciences. This book was composed, printed, and bound in the United States.

98   97   96   95   94   6   5   4   3   2   1

Library of Congress Cataloging-in-Publication Data
Religion, feminism, and freedom of conscience : a Mormon/humanist
    dialogue / edited by George D. Smith.
            p.   cm.
        ISBN 0-87975-887-2 (Prometheus)
        ISBN 1-56085-048-5 (Signature :pbk)
            1. Liberty of conscience—United States. 2. Freedom of religion—
        United States. 3. Mormon Church—Doctrines. 4. Church of Jesus
        Christ of Latter-day Saints—Doctrines. 5. Humanism 6. Feminist
        theory. 7. Academic freedom—United States. 8. Brigham Young
        University. 9. United States—Religion.   I. Smith, George D.
        BL2525.R4635   1994   94-8606
        323.44'2—dc20   CIP

Contents

Editor's Introduction   vii

Overview:
Humanism and the Idea of Freedom
Paul Kurtz   xvii

PART I. FREEDOM OF CONSCIENCE

1. The September Six
   Lavina Fielding Anderson   3

2. The Politics of Exclusivity
   Robert Alley   9

3. Secular and Religious Interpretations of Scripture
   Gerald A. Larue   17

4. Freedom of Conscience: Individual Right or
   Social Responsibility?
   L. Jackson Newell   31

PART II. ACADEMIC FREEDOM

5. Academic Freedom at Brigham Young University:
   Free Inquiry in Religious Context
   Allen Dale Roberts   43

6. A Humanist View of Religious Universities
   Vern L. Bullough   63

7. Academic Freedom Forever; However . . .
   Frederick S. Buchanan   73

8. Tenure as a Tool
   F. Ross Peterson   87

9. Religion and Academics at
    Brigham Young University:
    A Recent Historical Perspective
    Gary James Bergera   93

PART III. FEMINISM

10. A Feminist Comparison of Mormonism
    and Humanism
    Bonnie Bullough   117

11. The Struggle to Emerge: Leaving
    Brigham Young University
    Martha Sonntag Bradley   123

12. Dancing Through the Doctrine:
    Observations on Religion and Feminism
    Cecilia Konchar Farr   141

    Epilogue:
    The Indispensable Opposition (1939)
    Walter Lippmann   153

    Contributors   161

Editor's Introduction

On September 24, 1993, a gathering of secular humanists and members of the Church of Jesus Christ of Latter-day Saints (Mormons) met for three days in Salt Lake City, Utah, to discuss freedom of conscience as it applies to academic freedom and to expressions of feminism. For years both secular humanists and Mormons have endorsed freedom of conscience. What is open to debate is whether principles of what Mormons refer to as free agency apply to feminists and to teachers at Brigham Young University, which is owned by the Mormon church.

Freedom of conscience, the freedom of individuals to think and act as they believe, has been part of the social contract of societies which have sought to replace autocratic rule with various forms of self-government. Whereas dictatorial leaders might seek to direct the thoughts and activities of people within their domain of influence, documents such as the Magna Carta in England and the American Constitution sought to reserve for individuals certain rights, including the right to express their own beliefs and the freedom to act upon those beliefs.

The right, and some would assert, responsibility, of individuals to think, speak, write, and act as they consider to be appropriate and necessary—the right and responsibility to exercise their freedom of conscience—has played a significant role in democratic communities. Recent changes in Eastern Europe exemplify this process: where leadership could no longer enforce unpopular policy, revolution became irresistible. Institutions can and do change, sometimes peacefully, sometimes by revolution; the American people insisted on their freedom of conscience and broke away from the British Empire to become a nation.

The "liberty" that the Constitutional framers sought to guarantee to American citizens was incorporated into the First Amendment of the Bill of Rights, which states: "Congress shall make no law respecting the establishment of religion, or prohibiting the free exercise thereof; or abridging the freedom of speech, or of the press; or the right of the people peaceably to assemble, and to petition the government for a redress of grievances."

As a result of the overwhelming Mormon plurality in Utah and Congress's concerns about religious domination, the Utah constitution not only incorporates the freedoms of the Bill of Rights, but also includes added protection in its Article I, Section 4:

> The rights of conscience shall never be infringed. The state shall make no law respecting an establishment of religion or prohibiting the free exercise thereof; . . . there shall be no union of Church and State, nor shall any church dominate the State, or interfere with its functions. No Public money or property shall be appropriated for or applied to any religious worship, exercise or instruction, or for the support of any ecclesiastical establishment . . .

The balance between freedom and authority has always been difficult. Jean-Jacques Rousseau felt that governments should have only limited rights to regulate the behavior of individuals who contract to be part of that society. Ultimately, the authority of leaders depends on the willingness of individuals in a society or organization to accept that authority. Governmental authority derives from people who support a state with taxes and agree to obey its laws; ecclesiastical authority derives from congregations who agree to follow its edicts and to support its leaders financially.

Following a long tradition which evolved from Roman jurisprudence and developed in British Common Law, American courts have continually adjudicated the boundaries between appropriate state authority and the rights of individuals. Tensions between group and individual rights expressed in the current essays have a long historical tradition.

Issues of conscience versus state and church authority were articulated by such rebels as Socrates, Jesus, and Galileo. Socrates was a fifth-century philosopher and teacher of Athens, scholar of geometry and astronomy, veteran of the Peloponnesian War, legislator, and father of three sons. He helped lay the philosophical foundations of western culture, although he wrote nothing; his ideas are reflected in

Plato's dialogues and the writings of Xenophon. Impressed with the providential order of nature, as he saw it, he applied universal definitions and divisions to nature and developed a system of inductive reasoning. Socrates defined the "soul" as character and intelligence; he reasoned that happiness depended on the goodness of one's soul. When one "knows" true goodness, doing right is involuntary. Socrates followed this early argument for freedom of conscience to the point of political dissent, for which he was tried and condemned to death.

Jesus (Greek for Yeshua or Joshua) was the son of a Judean carpenter in a Roman colony at the edge of the empire. He became a teacher or rabbi and wandered through settlements in and around Galilee with twelve followers preaching religious reform, teaching by parable, and practicing healing. Jesus preached the redeeming love of God for every person regardless of social class. His attacks on hypocrisy and his indifference to wealth and status were well received by common people and opposed by the privileged. We would expect this reaction to any religious reformer who gathered the homeless and walked to the center of town assailing church leaders. Religious and political authorities alike accused him of being a revolutionary. Regarded by some as the long-awaited Messiah, Jesus was arrested by Roman soldiers, condemned as a blasphemer by the Sanhedrin—a Jewish council—and was crucified by the Roman procurator, Pontias Pilate. Christianity developed around belief in his resurrection from the dead.

Although, like Socrates, Jesus wrote nothing that is extant, various stories and narratives about him were written down and edited some time after his death. Among the writings considered by scholars to be most representative of what Jesus actually said are some of the parables. He taught that the letter of the law was an insufficient guide to ethical behavior; he rejected the legalistic actions of the Jewish Pharisees. Jesus was an advocate for the marginalized: heathens, Samaritans, publicans (tax collectors), and harlots. His parable of the Pharisee and the publican demonstrates his respect for humility over dogmatic obedience (Luke 18:10-14a). In his remarkable exercise of independent conscience which cost him his life, Jesus preached a universal message that offended the establishment of first-century Palestine.

Galileo Galilei, an early seventeenth-century professor of mathematics at the University of Padua, Italy, was an astronomer and physicist whose discoveries contradicted the moral authority of the Christian church. Considered one of the founders of the experimental method, he developed the astronomical telescope with which he discovered the satellites of Jupiter and learned that the Milky Way was composed of stars. From his observations and analysis he affirmed the Copernican theory, that the planets revolve around the sun, similar to a long-ignored theory of the third-century B.C.E. Greek astronomer, Aristarchus.

Although a member of the established church who had attended a monastery near Florence, Galileo could not deny what he knew: the earth revolves around the sun and is not the fixed center of the universe. When Dominican prelates denounced Galileo for blasphemy, he wrote to church authorities in Rome to remind them that, in the past, when the Bible conflicted with undeniable scientific truth, scripture had been interpreted allegorically. Quoting church dicta, he warned that it would be "a terrible detriment for the souls if people found themselves convinced by proof of something that it was made then a sin to believe." Galileo went to Rome to persuade the Pope to lift the ban on Copernicus's ideas. He was brought to trial before the Inquisition, interrogated, threatened with torture, and forced to recant. Although he spent the last eight years of his life under house arrest as punishment for having "held and taught" Copernican doctrine, he managed to finish his book *New Sciences* and smuggle it out to Protestants in the Netherlands. It was published in 1638, four years before Galileo died.

The struggles of Socrates, Jesus, and Galileo exemplify significant innovators of our civilization who expressed their freedom of conscience at great personal cost. The tradition of exercising freedom of conscience, of speaking truth to authority, was a primary theme of the Renaissance, when humanism was born. Often traced to the fourteenth-century Italian poet Petrarch, from whence it spread across western Europe, humanism elevated humanity's relationship to God. Humanism advocated free will and the capacity to understand and control nature. The mysteries of the sun, moon, stars, planets, rain, lightning and thunder, and the seemingly endless systems of plants and animals were now examined analytically and treated as subjects for humankind to study and understand.

The Renaissance inspired widespread interest in knowledge from advanced cultures of the past. As Augustine had years earlier sought to combine ancient Greek thought with Hebrew scriptures in a Christian synthesis of Plato and Moses, scholars now widely searched for ancient documents. This thirst for understanding began to challenge subservient reliance on both the state and received tradition.

By the nineteenth century humanism incorporated the positivist thinking of August Comte, which produced a value system independent of a belief in God. However, twentieth-century theologians such as Karl Barth asserted that the Christian gospel was part of humanism in that it taught that each person is uniquely created in the image of God.

From its outset humanism emphasized a questioning attitude, objective analysis of perceived experience, and respect for the dignity of humankind. An intelligence capable of critical scrutiny and self-inquiry was a "free intelligence." In his "Orations on the Dignity of Man," Italian philosopher Pico della Mirandola asserted that humanity had been assigned no fixed limit by God but was free to seek its own level and create its own future. With this focus on human thought and analysis, humanism embraced freedom of conscience.

Although religious thinkers advocated some of its principles, humanists inevitably found themselves on a collision course with religion. Humanism led scholars to the secular realm of science and mathematics, and to the pagan literature of Greece and Rome. Studies in these areas effectively eroded the territory of faith. Intellectual individualism challenged the Catholic church's presumption of universal authority. The church distrusted secular humanism because it entertained new ideas on their merits rather than judging them against a prescribed standard of belief.

While religious authority has often played a role in limiting freedom of conscience, many religious movements themselves could have been born only in a climate of freedom. The Mormon church arose and flourished in an atmosphere of toleration and freedom of conscience that the pluralistic society of nineteenth-century America provided. Mormon founder Joseph Smith and his early followers could not accept the principles of Christian churches practicing in

New York, Ohio, Missouri, and Illinois during the 1820s-40s. Specifically, these early Mormons rejected the doctrine of "original sin" by which errors of judgment attributed to biblical Adam impugned the dignity of all. Smith discarded the Christian notion that the Earth was created *ex nihilo*—out of nothing. Incorporating concepts of the Scientific Revolution, Smith believed that matter was eternal and that the earth must have been created out of existing elements in a cosmic reorganization. Furthermore, at a time when the biblical flat-earth scenario, with Heaven above and Hell below, had been rendered obsolete by Copernicus, Joseph Smith envisioned a creator living, not above sluice gates of rain in the "great dome," but on a separate planet. He attributed to this creator a natural progression from the status of human being, complete with spouse, parents and grandparents. In fact, Smith thought that every human being had the potential to become a god and rule a personal planet.

Smith went far afield from traditional Christianity and offended the sensibilities of neighbors. Illinois governor Thomas Ford listed the following causes of antagonism toward the Mormons: violations of freedom of the press, general religious views, polygamy, military strength, rumors of intent to destroy a nearby newspaper, Mormon alliance with native Americans, alleged coronation of Joseph Smith, vigilante bands, assertions that God had consecrated neighbors' property to Mormons, and bloc voting which made Mormon approval necessary for politicians (*History of Illinois* [1854], 2:166-76). Mormons were as different and undesirable to their mid-western neighbors as the Rajneesh was to Oregon or David Koresh to Texas. Mormons suffered what they considered to be deprivation of their rights, while their neighbors felt that their rights were threatened by the Mormons. However, it was internal dissent over the secret practice of polygamy in Illinois that, in large part, led to a chain of events which resulted in the death of the Mormon prophet and the expulsion of the Mormons from Illinois. Smith's followers left the United States to take refuge in the Great Salt Lake Valley (in Mexican territory at that time) where they felt they would be able to exercise religious freedom.

Following their migration to Utah, the Mormons modified their doctrines to gain public acceptance. In 1890 the church abandoned polygamy in exchange for eventual statehood in 1896. As recently as

1978, another dissonant doctrine was terminated, the disfranchisement of blacks for some postulated curse attributed to wrongdoing in a pre-earth existence. Mormons no longer preach that the end of the world is near or that they will soon occupy their neighbors' property and rule over them. But a century after freedom of conscience was invoked to form their radically new religion, the rhetoric of some Mormon leaders is ambivalent regarding the universality of such a right.

At a time when academic freedom is circumscribed by loyalty oaths and doctrinal hegemony at Brigham Young University, when Mormon scholars are excommunicated for discussing contradictions in historical documents, it is easy to forget that Mormon leaders have consistently embraced "free agency" as an essential principle of Mormon doctrine. Founder Joseph Smith said, "I teach the people correct principles and they govern themselves" (*Journal of Discourses* 10:57-58); also, "We are not disposed, had we the power, to deprive anyone of exercising . . . free independence of mind" (*Teachings of the Prophet Joseph Smith*, 49).

The importance of freedom is evidenced in Mormon scripture, which declares that freedom emanated from the mouth of God: "It is not meet that I should command in all things; for he that is compelled in all things, the same is slothful and not a wise servant" (Doctrine and Covenants 58:26-28). Further, "Every man may act in doctrine and principle . . . according to the moral agency which I have given unto him, that every man may be accountable for his own sins in the day of judgment" (Doctrine and Covenants 101:78). According to the Book of Mormon, one purpose of earth life is to allow eternal beings to make choices (2 Nephi 2:15-16). If forced to choose the right, a 1993 Mormon Sunday school lesson explained, we would not be able to demonstrate what we would choose for ourselves. The lesson suggested that the teacher put a cord around a child's arms and ask if he or she felt free (*Gospel Doctrine Sunday School* manual [1993], chap. 4, 18).

Jesus is often quoted in LDS sermons, "And ye shall know the truth, and the truth shall make you free" (John 8:32). Early Mormon apostle Orson Pratt preached that "All beings having intelligence must have their agency. Laws must be given, suited and adapted to this agency; and when God sends inhabitants on various creations he sends them on the great and grand principle of giving them an opportunity to exercise that agency (*Essential Orson Pratt* [1991], 374). Brigham Young agreed that freedom is "a law of [human] existence, and the Lord cannot violate his own law; were he to do that he would cease to be God . . . this is a law which has existed from all eternity, and will continue to exist throughout all the eternities to come. Every intelligent being must have the power of choice" (*Journal of Discourses* 11:272). Latter-day Saint president Joseph F. Smith wrote, "The Almighty raised up [this nation] . . . to the end that those who are kept in bondage and serfdom may be brought to the enjoyment of the fullest freedom and liberty of conscience possible for intelligent man to exercise in the earth" (*Gospel Doctrine* [1939], 409).

Some Mormons believe that political and religious liberty is critically important for the church today. Current LDS apostle Dallin Oaks has explained:

> The Church of Jesus Christ of Latter-day Saints does not attempt to isolate its members from alternate voices. Its approach, as counseled by the prophet Joseph Smith, is to teach correct principles and then leave its members to govern themselves by personal choices. Members of the church are free to participate or to listen to any alternate voices they choose, but church leaders should avoid official involvement directly or indirectly (*Ensign*, May 1989, 28).

Similarly, the current senior apostle of the LDS Quorum of the Twelve, Howard W. Hunter, reflected: "To fully understand this gift of agency and its inestimable worth, it is imperative that we understand that God's chief way of acting is by persuasion and patience and long-suffering, not by coercion and stark confrontation" (*Ensign*, Nov. 1989, 18).

Elder Loren C. Dunn of the LDS First Council of the Seventy endorsed freedom of conscience with these words: "No one will force us to do what is right. We should be 'in tune' with the spirit, that is, listen to our conscience, and then 'discipline ourselves'" (*This I Know* [1985], 6-7). Apostle Boyd K. Packer was asked by the wife of a U.S. Army general how Mormons are able to control their youth. He responded, "We develop control by teaching freedom . . . A four-star general is nothing if not a disciplinarian. But when one understands the Gospel, it becomes very clear that the best control is self control" (*Ensign*, May 1983).

The mutual heritage of freedom of conscience among Mormons and humanists provides common ground for dialogue. Although each group might not agree entirely on the meaning of religious and intellectual expression, they both understand and recognize the importance of freedom.

The present conflict in the Mormon community regarding academics and feminists is addressed in the essays contained in this volume. BYU faculty have been forbidden from participating in unapproved symposia and conferences. In 1992 Phi Beta Kappa for the third time in fifteen years denied permission to establish a chapter at BYU because its mission statement, which forbids academic work that contradicts fundamental church doctrines, is "problematic for an institution of higher learning where free inquiry should prevail" (*Salt Lake Tribune*, May 20, 1992). The 1995 accreditation process for BYU begins this year with self-evaluation by BYU administrators, and must be pursued with courage and integrity.

We hope that the Mormon community will recall its heritage as religious humanists, a heritage of freedom of conscience and expression that requires the community to find a way to listen to thoughtful dissenters and discuss differences with mutual respect. At the same time, secular humanists, with their tradition of tolerance and open-mindedness, will find that they have much in common and much to admire in the passion, honesty, and intellectual integrity of Mormons, as well as of people of other faiths who earnestly try to harmonize their religious and intellectual traditions.

Overview:
Humanism and
the Idea of Freedom

Paul Kurtz

I

This dialogue is historic, for as far as we are aware it is the first formal exchange of ideas by Mormons and humanists. In a pluralistic society, such as America, it is important that people from diverse religious and nonreligious traditions engage in debate to define differences and more meaningfully to discover common ground.

As a representative of humanism, I am often asked, What does the term "humanism," or indeed "secular humanism," mean? The latter term has been attacked by religious fundamentalists on the right for well over a decade. Can "humanism" be defined; or is it like Jell-O, as a friendly critic characterized it, in that it cannot be nailed to a tree or pinned down?

The term "humanism" means different things to different people. For some, it has been simply identified with the study of the "humanities." For others, it has been used synonymously with "humanitarianism." Its critics have condemned it as a mere form of "godless atheism." Some have considered humanism to be a new religion, and others a new form of anti-religion. Yet even critics would not consider themselves "anti-humanist." Like "democracy," "socialism," "peace," "motherhood," or "virtue," humanism is all things to all men and women.

Is there any way out of this definitioneering impasse? Humanism is not "an ideal essence," laid up in some Platonic heaven of abstract meanings. On the contrary, in unraveling its meaning we see that it has been used to justify a set of ethical principles. And in this linguistic controversy there is a central idea that emerges strongly, the idea of freedom. Throughout its long tradition of usage the term "humanism" has embodied the sense of freedom. In particular, humanists have wished to defend the values of the free mind, free inquiry, and free thought.

Humanism has had a long, though checkered, career in human history. Indeed, it is one of the oldest and deepest intellectual traditions of Western civilization. From the great philosophers, scientists, poets, and artists of the Greek and Roman world, through the Renaissance, to the development of the New Science in the sixteenth century, the discovery of the New World, and the democratic revolutions of the modern era, the basic humanist value of *liberty* has inspired the noble deeds and passions of countless men and women.

The first principle of humanism, thus, is its commitment to the idea of freedom. But what does this mean? First, freedom of conscience within the inward domain of thought and belief; second, the free expression of ideas; and third, freedom of choice in the moral domain. These ideas have been central to American democracy and were among the most cherished of the Founding Fathers. Thomas Jefferson, author of the Declaration of Independence, affirmed his opposition to any tyranny over the human mind. And James Madison, chief architect of the Constitution and the Bill of Rights, affirmed that government should make no law abridging freedom of speech or press, or prohibiting the free exercise of religion. American democracy protects all forms of belief.

Humanism and libertarianism are thus indelibly intertwined. Humanists in the modern world have been the chief critics of the authoritarian or totalitarian state. John Stuart Mill, John Dewey, Karl Popper, Sidney Hook, and others have provided a powerful case in defense of democracy. Indeed, the first opponents of fascism and communism are humanist intellectuals who defend the open society.

What is often overlooked in this debate is that liberty may be endangered by other powerful institutions in society which *de facto* tend to limit the inward domain of conscience, freedom of expression, and moral freedom. I have in mind many established churches, temples, or mosques which may seek to deny the most fundamental of all human rights: primacy of conscience and the right to believe *or* not to believe. This is especially evident in Muslim countries today, where there is no separation between church and state, and theocracies repress human freedom. In the name of Allah, Salman Rushdie (an avowed secular humanist) was condemned to death by Iranians as a blasphemer; no one is permitted to dissent from prevailing Islamic doctrines. Extremist Muslim fundamentalists do not simply excommunicate; they seek to execute! In the history of religious persecution, the Roman Catholic Inquisition no doubt stands out as an infamous illustration of the worst-case scenario. But even where there is separation of church and state, churches may have powerful influences on adherents, demanding absolute obedience. The threat of excommunication, the censorship of publications, or the limits imposed on professors are unfortunate illustrations of the power of some churches seeking to enforce discipline in a community. Does a church in a free society have a legal right to do that? Does it have a moral right, particularly in a pluralistic democracy? A similar question can be asked of powerful economic forces: the coercive sanctions imposed by a corporation or a company town on its employees, or perhaps a union on its members.

In his famous work *On Liberty* John Stuart Mill presents a set of arguments as to why the rights of the minority need to be respected, including the rights of heretics, dissenters, or iconoclasts. For Mill, the real question is, How do you deal with the tyranny of the majority? Namely, if a majority of people in the community fervently believe that something is true, do they have a right to exercise coercion, whether subtle or overt, in order to demand conformity to the prevailing orthodoxy? Mill argues that people who deny freedom imply that they are infallible and/or that they have a monopoly of truth or virtue. But who can say with assurance that his or her beliefs have reached their final formulation, and that they alone have the Absolute truth? Is not truth a product of the give-and-take of a free marketplace of ideas, and does it not depend on criticism and response to that criticism if it is to prevail? One should always leave open the possibility that one may be mistaken. Surely the very premise of democracy is that we have something to learn from those who disagree with us. But, says Mill, even if we believe we have the Absolute truth, not to allow it to be contested by dissenters would mean that it would degenerate into a mere habit of thought. It would lose all conviction and vitality for succeeding generations—unless it were allowed to be challenged. Those who deny freedom of inquiry perhaps mask a hidden fear that if there were really an open debate, they would lose in the end. The censor or inquisitor thus seeks to unfairly impose his or her views by insisting on conformity by everyone.

The point is, quasi-public institutions, such as the Church, Corporation, University, or even public opinion, may be as powerful as the government, and individuals should have the right to dissent in the face of such power. Perhaps the strongest argument in favor of freedom of conscience, free expression, and free inquiry is that these freedoms will, in the long run, contribute to the public good and to the progressive development of knowledge, for they allow for the emergence of creativity and the uncovering of new dimensions of truth. By closing the parameters of dissent, the quest for knowledge is restricted. Given the great problems that humankind constantly faces, it is essential that new avenues for the discovery of knowledge be encouraged.

The most awesome attack on freedom in our time was in Marxist-Leninist-Stalinist societies. During the long night of communism, a reign of intellectual terror prevailed, and anyone who disagreed with or defied the doctrine of dialectical materialism was severely punished. If Salman Rushdie stands as the symbol today of the status of freedom in the Islamic world, so Andrei Sakharov, who was a great exponent of secular humanist ideals, symbolizes the yearning for freedom in former Soviet society.

II

Permit me to apply the idea of freedom very briefly to three areas that we will explore during this dialogue. First, to the question of academic freedom in the university; second, to the scientific investigation of religion; and third, to the area of women's rights.

The university is a unique institution in society, for it has a double function. On the one hand, it is interested in transmitting to students the best knowledge available within civilization and in cultivating an appreciation for the quest for knowledge. This is known as *Lernfrei-*

heit; that is, it is the right of students to learn and to be able to engage in free inquiry. Students at a university are thus placed in contact with the best minds and the best literature in many domains of human experience and knowledge. They have a right to cultural freedom without censorship or prohibition. The university, however, is especially unique because it is the primary institution committed not only to teaching but to research. Here we need to distinguish the college from the multiversity. What is preeminent is that the university is not only a repository of wisdom and truth in all the fields of human endeavor, but that it provides fertile soil where professors and researchers can come together and explore cooperatively the quest for knowledge. This is what *Lernfreiheit* presupposes, as its basic principle, academic freedom. Thus universities seek to appoint to their faculties the best qualified minds who are competent in their fields and recognized by peers. A university must give to its faculty the freedom to pursue research, to reach conclusions which, on the basis of their considered judgments, seem to be true, and this entails the right to speak out and publish the results. Any effort by the corporate body to censor or to prohibit this is to deny *Lernfreiheit*, and this is a betrayal of the very idea of the university itself. Academic freedom has a long and distinguished career, and the great universities—from Oxford, Cambridge, the Sorbonne to Harvard, Stanford, and state universities—respect this right. This not only applies to secular, but increasingly to religious institutions as well.

Authoritarian institutions fear new ideas; they persecute intellectuals; and they seek to deny tenure to their professors. Is there a necessary contradiction between an ecclesiastical institution and a university such that an ecclesiastical institution need not permit *Lernfreiheit*? If this is the case, then a viable university no longer can be said to exist, and the university has become a place for indoctrination, a seminary; it is not receptive to the quest for truth, nor does it respect the right of dissent. Humanists, of course, will not compromise on this point. To declare an institution a university entails academic freedom untrammeled by the threats of a Grand Inquisitor.

The second theme that we will focus on in this dialogue is the question of what should be the extent or limits placed on freedom of inquiry in regard to religious doctrines. It is again the conviction of the humanist that every domain of human interest, whether economics or politics, the social sciences, natural, or biological sciences, history, literature, philosophy, the arts, or religion, should be amenable to critical investigation. This means that there should be no blocks placed on free inquiry. It means that the Koran, the Bible, or the Book of Mormon should be read like any other book, using the best tools of scientific, linguistic, and scholarly research, and that any claims made in these books can be examined critically and evaluated cognitively.

Now there are those who are opposed to this, and who believe that this kind of free inquiry would endanger faith, upset dogma, imperil the body of church doctrines. That may or may not be the case. Surely, if one has little hope that an analysis of belief will survive critical scrutiny, or if one believes that questioning beliefs will lead to their destruction, then so much the worse for the beliefs. If we are truly convinced that our beliefs are true, we ought to permit them to be challenged. And that is why in the area of biblical or Koranic or Mormon criticism, the most advanced tools of scientific, historical, and scholarly analysis should be employed.

The third area for discussion in this dialogue is the question of human rights: to what extent should they be extended to women? Are not women equal in dignity and value? Do not the interests and needs of women deserve equal consideration with those of men? Or should the role of women in various institutions of society be relegated to a submissive position? It is clear that patriarchal attitudes have long dominated our social institutions. The battle of the suffragist movement for the vote gave women political equality. Similarly for the great battles in the economy and in the university today where there is a need to allow women to achieve positions of responsibility. The real question is, Do not the *same* considerations apply to religious institutions? There are some religions today that believe that women should serve in the pulpit to the same extent as men; that the viewpoints of women are entitled to be heard; that their freedoms should be protected and encouraged; other religions deny this. Is God the Father a male and is sexist language tolerable in a religious context? Humanists agree with the feminist indictment, and indeed many outstanding leaders of the feminist movement worldwide have been humanists, such as Betty Friedan, Gloria Steinem, and Simone de Beauvoir. Hence, the cause of women for liberation is continuous with the cause of freedom.

III

The concluding point I wish to raise briefly is the commitment of humanists to reason. Humanists believe that it is essential that we encourage the tools of critical thinking in society. Belief should not simply be a question of faith or dogma, emotion or intuition, custom or authority, but should be guided by informed judgment, an appeal to evidence and logic, and tested in practice. Humanists maintain that there are areas of reliable knowledge that we share, and that truth is not established by authoritative declaration but by objective justification.

Thus the idea of freedom as a humanist value is concomitant with the idea of reason, and humanism may also be defined by its commitment to a method of rational inquiry. It is our conviction that we ought to engage in a dialogue with those with whom we disagree, and that we ought not to seek to impose our views on others by power or force, but we ought to listen in a fair and impartial way to claims made in the free marketplace of ideas, and that we ought to try to work out the best we can what seems most likely true on the basis of cooperative, rational inquiry. This is what the following Mormon/humanist dialogue is all about.

Part I
Freedom of Conscience

1.
The September Six

Lavina Fielding Anderson

During the month of September 1993 six Mormon scholars in Utah, representing both liberal and conservative ends of the spectrum, were served with notices by ecclesiastical leaders to appear before church courts, called disciplinary councils, to answer charges of apostasy or conduct unbecoming members of the church. By the end of September five of these men and women were excommunicated (expelled) from the LDS church and one woman was disfellowshipped (forbidden to participate in church activities). The church denied that it had conducted a purge.

I am one of these September Six. The issue over which my disciplinary council was held could have been the evaluation of historical facts, as was the case of D. Michael Quinn (excommunicated), or feminism, as it was in the cases of Maxine Hanks (excommunicated) and Lynne Whitesides (disfellowshipped), though probably not theology, as in the cases of Paul Toscano (excommunicated) and Avraham Gileadi (excommunicated). Instead, the cause of action in my proceeding was my discussion of ecclesiastical abuse—church leaders exercising "unrighteous dominion" (D&C 121:39) over members. If I may appropriate a phrase from another context, the shortest definition of ecclesiastical abuse is what Paul Edwards, a scholar of the Reorganized Church of Jesus Christ of Latter Day Saints, terms "the Sumo Wrestling School of Administration," which he defines as "throwing your weight around while trying to cover your rear."[1]

---

1. See D. Michael Quinn, *Early Mormonism and the Magic World View*

Abuse occurs when any church officer, acting in his calling and using the weight of his office, coerces compliance, imposes his personal opinions as church doctrine or policy, or resorts to such power plays as threats and intimidation to insure that his personal views prevail in a conflict of opinions. The suggestion is always made that the member's faith is weak, testimony inadequate, and commitment to the church lacking.

Seven factors characterize the most abusive encounters:

(1) A difference of opinion is not treated simply as that, but as a sign of moral inadequacy. If the difference stems from a member's scholarship or involves application of professional tools to an aspect of Mormon studies, the officer may lack the technical expertise to discuss the point at issue and frequently shifts the discussion to the dangers of promulgating any perspective but the traditional one. He often insists that there is something wrong with alternative views.

(2) A request for help is seen as an invitation to judge a member's worthiness.

(3) No matter what the content of the initial issue, *any* issue can escalate into a power struggle in which the ecclesiastical officer demands compliance because of his office and accuses the member of not sustaining his leaders and/or of apostasy. These charges, in turn, lead to threats to confiscate temple recommends, to release the member from local responsibilities, and to conduct disciplinary councils which could result in temporary disfellowshipment or excommunication.

(4) If the member protests such actions and refuses to yield to intimidation, then the very act of protest is seen as further evidence

---

(Salt Lake City: Signature Books, 1989) and his study on Mormon hierarchy forthcoming from Signature Books. Lynne Whitesides is president of the Mormon Women's Forum. See Paul and Margaret Toscano, *Strangers in Paradox* (Salt Lake City: Signature Books, 1987); Avraham Gileadi, *The Last Days: Types and Shadows from the Bible and the Book of Mormon* (Salt Lake City: Deseret Book, 1991); Paul M. Edwards, "A Comment on the Writing of Ethics," in *Distinguished Author Lectures, 1988-1989*, Roger Yarrington, ed., (Independence, MO: Herald House, 1989), 1:13.

of rebellion. The officer unilaterally terminates discussion by citing his authority. The member, rather than having a problem, has become the problem.

(5) If another ecclesiastical leader such as a stake president or an area president becomes aware of the situation, the original leader controls the flow of information to him. The opportunities to present biased information, reframe the issue as one of disobedience, and portray the member as a trouble-maker are legion. The first leader seldom suggests a group discussion or meeting that involves a mediator or referee; rather, he is usually able to use the weight of the second officer's authority to reinforce his own in the effort to force capitulation.

(6) The member naturally feels unjustly treated. Feelings of helplessness, betrayal, anger, and depression frequently follow. Expressions of "increased love" (D&C 121:43) seldom if ever follow "rebukes," only additional warnings about conformity that increase the sense of powerlessness in the face of unfair treatment.

(7) If the member withdraws in pain from church activity to protect himself, herself, and/or the family from this assault upon their spiritual well-being, the withdrawal is seen as evidence of the member's deficiency, not as a cry for help or as a symptom of an abusive system.

In the spring 1993 issue of *Dialogue: A Journal of Mormon Thought* I documented over a hundred cases of ecclesiastical abuse directed primarily at scholars and historians. Since then, over a hundred ordinary members of the church have come forward with their own experiences of injustice, usually suffered in silence, bewilderment, and anguish. Such abuse is not a social or political problem for me. It is a spiritual one—a matter of conscience. I consider myself to be a believing and orthodox Mormon. Hence, I speak now from the center of my religious tradition, using the language of my religion. Two scriptures have run repeatedly through my mind: "He is despised and rejected of men; a man of sorrows, and acquainted with grief: and we hid as it were our faces from him; he was despised, and we esteemed him not" (Isa. 53:3). That is what happened to so many of the people I have talked to—decent, ordinary members of the church have been despised and esteemed not. And the second one, "Inasmuch as ye have done it unto one of the least of these my brethren, ye have done it unto me" (Matt. 25:40). Ecclesiastical abuse spoke directly to my conscience and I answered it.

I have pondered the unmistakable reality of this abusive intolerance carefully and prayerfully for over two years, ever since a joint council of the LDS First Presidency and Quorum of Twelve Apostles, the highest-ranking administrative bodies in the LDS church hierarchy, issued a statement against unofficial symposia. I certainly knew it was risky to voice dissent, since our church has a long history of shooting the messenger that brings unpleasant news. I never received any spiritual guarantees that I would be safe or that the church would welcome the news and change quickly, but I did receive over and over again the assurance that it was the right thing to do. That assurance has been the single most important factor in the strength I have felt at every step of this process. I was impressed that in the scores of letters I have received expressing love and support, the person who spoke most directly and most insightfully to the issue of conscience was not a Mormon at all, but a Catholic friend, who said: "I have in my life done a few costly things for the sake of my conscience, and I am proudest of them. May it be so for you" (Freda M. De Pillis to Lavina Fielding Anderson, 20 Sept. 1993).

As I gathered with a few friends on 23 September 1993, while the disciplinary council met without me a few blocks away, we ate popcorn and guacamole dip, exchanged the latest rumors and news, and watched *A Man for All Seasons*. Fred Buchanan, whose own essay is included in this compilation, had been working in his yard and felt compelled to join us. He drove over to the house and walked in, his face pale and stricken with sadness. As he tried to express his sympathy for me, I said, "How many times in our lives do we get to take a stand on a question of conscience? So much of what we do is choosing degrees of political correctness or balancing ethical standards against social constraints, or being 'reasonable' or 'realistic.' I feel *lucky*. This is a privilege that doesn't come to everyone." I did not realize, until I said those words, how deeply I meant and felt this. I also did not realize until I received the notice of excommunication the next morning that, no matter how well prepared I was or how carefully chosen my commitment, the blow would be so heavy.

I believe that the main issue is a struggle for the soul of Mormonism. Against a religion that has increasingly become a multiplication of forms and observances, catechisms and orthodoxies, the exuberant expansiveness of Mormon theology presents itself with vitality and vigor. Both the gospel of Jesus and Mormon doctrine teach love as the basis of human relations, liberation from all limitations, and an absolutely irreducible respect for human dignity and freedom. Ecclesiastical intimidation, silencing, and punishment violate these principles in every way. And it is the principles that will ultimately triumph—cracking, crumbling, and sweeping aside shameful practices that have their basis in fear, not love.

Historian Karl C. Sandberg points out that the terminology change from "church court" to "disciplinary council" may have had unexpected significance:

> "Courts" depend on a body of law and interpretation of the law, since very few cases are exact replicas of previous ones. The law is cumbersome, but it is written down and says that like cases must be treated in the manner of like precedents. It is the ultimate protection for the individual.
>
> To "discipline," on the other hand, is "to train by instruction and practice, especially to teach self-control to; to teach to obey rules or accept authority . . . ; to punish in order to gain control or to enforce obedience; to impose order on" (American Heritage Dictionary). . . . Every organization needs to exercise discipline (maintain order) to accomplish its purposes. The question to be raised here and to be reviewed periodically is this: does the shift away from "court" to "discipline" connote a shift away from the law, which protects the individual, to control and enforced obedience, which protect the institution? It seems to me to be an open and fruitful question ("Mormonism and the Puritan Connection: The Trials of Mrs. Anne Hutchinson and Several Persistent Questions Bearing on Church Governance," 12-13, forthcoming in *Sunstone*).

In 2 Timothy 1:7, the apostle Paul encouraged the young bishop Timothy with these words: "For God hath not given us the spirit of fear; but of power, and of love, and of a sound mind." Recently, fifteen good men, sincerely desiring to do the will of God, sat in judgement on my membership in the LDS church. If any of them had read this scripture, I wonder how they would have interpreted it. I know how it speaks to me.

When the histories of this turbulent period are written, I think historians will conclude that the Mormon church was wracked and rent by a spirit of fear, acting out a nightmare that took the form of scapegoating six of its own. Ecclesiastical officers have exercised, not godly power, but unrighteous dominion. Kindly and loving as individuals, they have collectively acted in punitive and unloving anger. Instead of manifesting sound judgement, they have stereotyped, demonized, and spurned. By their actions, they have demeaned the community they have been called to represent and the values of free agency their institution proclaims.

I have made many mistakes of my own and have contributed to the mistakes of others, but I know in my bones that it is no mistake now to call for a return to the gospel of Jesus, to call for greater love, forgiveness, and reconciliation in our community. Healing can occur in and be extended from whole individuals only, not from those who are codependent on an abusive institution. Ecclesiastical abuse must be addressed and solved. Certainly some organizational and structural changes will do much toward providing a sorely missing system of checks and balances. But the real protection of members lies in their own sense of empowerment, in an individual sense of duty to God rather than to the institution, and in the primacy of individual conscience.

2.
The Politics of Exclusivity

Robert Alley

Recently while visiting a zoo I thought once again of myself as a young boy wondering why Noah was always pictured as standing on the deck of the ark, until my brother informed me that with only one window there was good reason to stay there the entire trip. This evoked a thought about sincerity and the absurd.

There used to be a group called the British Flat Earth Society. It still exists, but it was once a vigorous operation. Then astronauts took themselves to the outer limits, circled the moon, and came back with photographs of the earth. When those photographs were published, the Flat Earth Society lost half its members. The half that pulled out must have believed the earth was flat or they could not have been convinced by a photograph. They were waiting for proof. They may have been in the backwaters of science, but at least they were finally persuaded.

In the late 1930s I used to listen to a half-hour radio program called "Music and the Spoken Word," by Richard L. Evans, broadcast from the Mormon Tabernacle on Temple Square in Salt Lake City. As I tuned in the program on Sunday mornings, I listened to the "spoken word" more than to the music. My father preferred the music. He was a Baptist minister and editor of a Baptist newspaper. He went to church and sat in the pew with the rest of us. One day I said to him, "It seems to me that Mr. Evans makes more sense than any preacher. Why do we go to church when this fellow from Salt Lake City sounds like he's making sense?" Caring concepts were evident in Evans's words. He was not promoting anything other than goodwill and decency as far as I could tell.

I have always appreciated my father's response: "We go to church because that is a part of what we believe. But I will admit you are learning more from that gentleman on the radio than from the preacher we hear every Sunday morning."

Earlier in his career my father had a church in a small Virginia town called Blackstone. He was a very intelligent, caring father who taught me many things about truth. But he got in trouble with his church because as he read the Bible he concluded that what he found there must not be forced on other people. He argued that missionary activity was, in many ways, an erroneously conceived practice. He felt it was the not the role of a believer to force his or her definitions on someone else.

He was of course not the first person to think that. In fact, in the Baptist tradition Roger Williams had said it long before. I respected that conclusion. I learned to doubt in the context of the Christian faith as my father understood it.

There are a lot of people like me who bring to our generation a heritage of respect and reverence for tradition. I recently listened to Sarah Weddington speak in San Francisco. She began by talking about her father, a Methodist minister, and what he taught her. I think it's important to put in context what the Bible means to us and to people who hold it in reverence. I challenge those who say the Bible is a book of magic to be forced on others. Once as I listened to Billy Graham, he said, "If the Bible told me that two and two were five, I'd believe it." I expect he would. But the Bible is not absurd for the people who wrote it; it becomes absurd when people in our day insist on taking it literally.

The Bible does not present us with material that is ridiculous in the context from which it came. The Bible springs from the context in which people then were thinking, searching, and trying to find answers. Although they did not find answers to our satisfaction, their efforts do not make them ridiculous.

Western religions have two components which when combined create problems. One is identification of a sacred text. Such a text can be different things, but for my tradition it is the Hebrew and Christian scriptures. For all too many that sacred text becomes an infallible book that is treated differently from all other books. It is usually bound in black with gold-colored leaves making it appear holy. This sacred text is the same that convinced one group of Protestants to drown another in the name of true baptism.

When you combine this sacred text with the belief that one's group alone has a unique revelation, then you can say to others, "With all due respect, my good friends, God does not hear your prayers because you do not believe as I do." Why do they say that? Because they combine an infallible book with unique revelation and think they have become God's chosen people. They want us to believe that they alone are God's and know how to interpret the Bible, since God cannot speak for herself. These presumptions of *sacred text* and *unique revelation* combine to create an arrogance of faith that is arguably the most destructive force in the world. It has gone on for centuries and it continues. Persecution, anger, and bitterness are carried out in the name of God.

Last week in San Francisco, after a talk about church and state matters, one knowledgeable gentleman asked about my belief in natural rights. I had been discussing the beliefs of Thomas Jefferson and James Madison. Jefferson spoke in glowing terms of natural rights. In 1777 he affirmed that if any future legislature should in any way overturn the guarantee of religious freedom, it should know it was violating fundamental, natural rights. The gentleman in San Francisco asked me, "What's the difference between natural rights and Christian faith? Aren't they both based on belief?" The answer is, "Yes." Jefferson could not prove there were natural rights. Nor could he prove there were only a few. He picked them out, said, "These are they," and built a structure of freedom based on them.

What can we observe about those principles? The best we can say is that they were better than Jefferson, for he did not free slaves, did not give women the vote, did not care too much about native Americans. But his constitutional views, reflected in the work of James Madison, set forth a document based on principles that continue to evolve. It seems to me that the test of the natural rights theory lies not in a pragmatic test, but in what it does for us as human beings.

We are the better because of a constitution that goes beyond the spirit of the men who wrote it. Most often, in contrast, Christianity is restrictive, overly concerned about the "original intent" of its authors. But the Constitution contains the germ of an idea that allows expansion, going beyond what its founders thought. That is humanism. Humanism affirms, "There is something good even holy in the human spirit." However we define humanism, whatever we say about it, the important thing is that it makes us better. I defy anyone to tell me that the shenanigans of churches across the land over the last several centuries in the name of original intent has made anyone the better for its inquisitions and crusades.

What was the Bible to the people who wrote it? To me, the Bible is not a text for faith. It is a record of religious encounters from people who wrote seriously. I think that they were probably like most of us today. They had a sense of what they believed and wrote about it. We may look back and say, "We don't accept that." But we should not make fools of them by assuming they acted like Jerry Falwell. I think that we need to respect the biblical writers because they were seeking answers and so are we. But we need not respect those who grab the Bible, turn those early writers into idiots, and then insist that we become a part of their movement.

On Christmas 1977 I visited a Unitarian church. At that time I chaired a university religion department. In one part of the chapel was a theist corner and in another an atheist corner. I was invited to speak to the atheist corner. They wanted to know why Christians were always trying to convert them. During that meeting I stated that the problem with Christianity was that it distorted the words of Jesus and turned him into a god. Thus Christians do not have to pay attention to what he said. Christianity only requires that its adherents believe he is divine. "Jesus never claimed to be God," I said.

The next day I found my father sitting in his chair, reading the newspaper, with a big headline: "'Jesus never claimed to be God,' says Professor Alley." This banner headline ran across the whole front page of the second section of the newspaper. My father said, "This is trouble." I said, "No. Who can bother me? I have tenure." I had served on the committee that wrote our tenure policy three years before.

Baptists take the view that there is autonomy in the local church and that freedom exists to that extent. If you are a member of the local church and say what you want to, nobody can do anything to you except the local church, which can throw you out. Lacking ecclesiastical power, Baptist preachers in my hometown were not happy with my statement and let it be known by calling me all kinds of names. They told me I was going to hell, and, as a matter of a fact,

Jerry Falwell said I should be kicked out of the back door of my school because I was not worthy to be kicked out the front.

Baptists were on the march. The president of the university began to meet with me regularly. He finally told me I couldn't be fired because I had tenure. He added that if we didn't do something about the situation, take the initiative, he might lose his position. He wasn't joking. I trusted the president, a good and decent man, a Baptist. He was worried about the school and his office. We discussed what to do and it was suggested I assume a new title, Professor of American Studies. I accepted this lateral move.

Some members of the trustees were angry about the event. My friends and colleagues urged that I not make an issue here that would destroy the school. Maybe they were right, maybe they were wrong in that concern. But they were genuinely worried that if I just stood and said, "I'm not budging," the president would have to leave and the school would be in serious trouble.

I called the American Academy of University Professors. I was then serving as president of the Virginia Conference of the AAUP. They said, "It's a religion question. We don't want to make any calls on this one. You could be in trouble because there are certain rights that the school has about this." They advised me to settle. I saw their stance as pathetic and cowardly, but it was what they told me. They felt the situation was more problematic than a simple question of academic freedom. In those circumstances I said to the president that if, in fact, a refusal by me to negotiate would damage the university, then I would accept the new title and continue to teach religion. It was understood that there was no question of my complete academic freedom in the new position. It was settled.

Since I knew this would not be easy to get past the trustees, I warned the president, "You know I'm going to continue to say that Jesus never claimed to be God. You're aware of that?"

He said, "I know. But maybe from now on it'll only appear in the TV pages of the newspaper."

The interesting thing in this story is what the college president then said to me. He asked if that were true why hadn't he ever heard it?

I said, "What do you mean?"

He said that the same professors that taught me this at Southern

Baptist Theological Seminary never mentioned it when they came to his Kentucky church to preach.

I explained, "I know they didn't because most told us, 'Keep this among ourselves, guys. Don't go out and tell the people in the pew what you think. You'll get in trouble.'"

This to me has been the problem for a long time. People who know better keep acting as though they do not know anything. Preachers who know what I'm talking about perpetuate a mythology of ignorance and then wonder why things like this occur. What churches sometimes do in the name of truth and decency turns both of these words to ashes.

Toward the end of the nineteenth century and beginning of the twentieth century some liberal Christian humanists said, "There's something wrong in interpreting Jesus according to the apostle Paul. It's not gospel-oriented." Then came new voices who spoke of the unity of the Bible, seeking to impose a Christian theology on the Bible before it was a text. These scholars—most of whom were good men—had an agenda to support their own theology. So Neo-Orthodoxy emerged certain it had nothing to fear from scholarship. But that was not true, and Neo-Orthodoxy collapsed when scholarship took it beyond where it wanted to go. Once you take the first step toward critical analysis of the Bible, you are on a road to destruction if you are committed to an orthodoxy based on ignorance and blindness. Religious freedom is something we possess as a political community. We insist that the religious freedom we hold dear be cherished throughout this country.

James Madison spoke of the danger of democracy as the "tyranny of the majority": the majority frequently violates all of the principles of democracy we hold dear. He was convinced that the main thing was to keep the various competing groups divided. That is where humanism is most likely to flourish. It does not prosper in dictatorships. It does not flourish in most churches. It grows where people are free. Jefferson and Madison knew that in order to keep them free, you must insist that the majority not take away the rights of the minority. That is something most churches seem never to understand.

Since 1962 the Supreme Court has silenced school-sponsored classroom prayers. That is a silence with enormous power. This silence protects the most precious possession of every citizen: human conscience. It is a resounding silence in the name of freedom and equality for every child without regard to belief or persuasion. It might be argued that the American cultural legacy is a reasoned governmental silence in the arena of speech and conscience that spawns the untamed rough-and-tumble of debate over ideals. This is the genius of our democratic heritage. Multiple cultures and religions are secure as long as none is allowed preeminence. The roots of democratic freedom lie neither in dogma nor doctrine, but in our common constitutional heritage of a secular, humanist republic.

3.
Secular and Religious Interpretations of Scripture

Gerald A. Larue

My intent is to compare secular and religious interpretations of Jewish scriptures, writings Christians title "The Old Testament." The word "old" is pejorative and connotes a prelude to superior Christian scriptures, "The New Testament." I use a term employed by Jewish scholars to identify their sacred writings: Ta-Na-K—which stands for Torah (Law), Nebhiim (Prophets), and Kethub-him (Writings).

My approach is three-fold: literary-historical, archaeological, and what I call "common sense" analysis. Even as I employ critical methodology, I am aware that for many the literature under consideration is accepted as a divinely revealed holy work to be treated as separate and apart from secular writings. Indeed, the Torah is considered to constitute the foundation of Judaism, embodying regulations revealed to Moses. Both Jews and Christians approach these writings seeking understanding of their religious heritage, insight into the nature of God, and guidance and succor for life. Many Jews and Christians do not engage in critical analysis. When questions arise, they are answered by denominational leaders from a faith position rather than from the findings of scholars.

Nevertheless, Tanak is literature and subject to various forms of literary-historical analysis.[1] It is important to note that critical

---

1. The scriptures of the Church of Jesus Christ of Latter-day Saints,

analyses are not employed uniquely by secular researchers, but from the beginning have been developed and used by religious savants.

The literary-historical approach to Tanak, which has been conducted primarily by religious scholars, seeks to determine when and where a writing was produced, by whom, for whom, and under what circumstances. The inquirer seeks to determine the kind of writing involved, to discern whether the document is a letter, a sermon, a fable, and so forth. Biblical scholar William Dever notes that as a result of literary analysis

> It has been demonstrated that the Bible is a composite of diverse genres including myths, folktales, epics, prose and poetic narratives, court annals, nationalistic propaganda, historical novellas, genealogies, cult legends, liturgical formulas, songs and psalms, private prayers, legal *corpora*, oracles and prophecy, homily and didactic materials, *belle lettres*, erotic poetry, apocalyptic and so on.[2]

Now that is quite a list! It warns us not to approach biblical writings uncritically and simply as divinely revealed history.

Biblical literary analysis began about 500 C.E. when a Jewish scholar, writing in the Talmud, challenged the claim that Moses wrote the entire Torah or Pentateuch—the first five books of the Bible. He noted that the final eight verses of Deuteronomy not only described Moses' death and burial but claimed that "there has not risen a prophet since in Israel like Moses." He suggested that "Joshua wrote . . . eight verses of the law" (*Baba Bathra* 14b-15a).

Over the centuries, Bible readers found other discrepancies in the Torah. They noted that despite Jewish and Christian belief in Mosaic authorship, nowhere does the Torah make this claim. In

---

notably the Book of Mormon, are also subject to such inquiry. See Brent Lee Metcalfe, ed., *New Approaches to the Book of Mormon: Explorations in Critical Methodology* (Salt Lake City: Signature Books, 1993).

2. William G. Dever, "Archaeology and the Bible," *Biblical Archaeology Review* 16 (May/June 1990), 3:52-58. For an extended discussion of the relationship between the Bible and archaeology, see Dever, *Recent Archaeological Discoveries and Biblical Research* (Seattle: University of Washington Press, 1990).

response, Christians pointed out that in the gospels Jesus made reference to "the things Moses commanded"; obviously Jesus believed that Moses was the author (Matt. 8:4, Mark 1:44, and so on).

But there were other problems. In Genesis 14:14 Abram is said to have led a group of men to the city of Dan; but Dan did not come into being until the time of the judges (Jdg. 18:29). The fundamentalist Christians argue that a later editor wanted to make clear that the Canaanite city of Laish of the time of Abram was the same as the Hebrew city of Dan. This explanation simply added to the evidence that some scribe had tampered with Moses' words.

A number of passages refer to places located "beyond the Jordan" which is to say on the east side of the Jordan River (cf. Gen. 50:10, Num. 35:14, Deut. 1:1, 5, 3:8, 4:46). Obviously the writers of those words were located on the western side, in Israel, a land that Moses never entered (Deut. 34).

Could Moses, as author, contradict himself? According to Numbers 35:6-7, the Levites were to receive territorial inheritances, but Deuteronomy 18:1 makes it clear that they were to have no inheritance. According to Exodus 3:13-15 and Exodus 6:2-3, the personal name of the deity, "Yahweh," was revealed for the first time to Moses on the holy mountain. Prior to this revelation, Yahweh was known only as "Elohim" or "El Shaddai." But Genesis 4:26 indicates that early patriarchs employed the personal name of the deity, "Yahweh" (cf. Gen. 22:14, 26:25, 27:20, 28:13). Would a single writer make so many contradictory statements?

Scholars soon came to realize that Moses did not write the Torah but that a number of writers, whose handiwork can be recognized and traced, contributed to the first five books of the Bible. It also became clear that the initial writings in the Torah did not originate when the Hebrews were wandering about in the desert, but began in the tenth century B.C.E. during the reign of Solomon. The final editing of the Torah was done during the fifth century B.C.E. During the 500 years between the Solomonic period and the final editing in the time of Ezra, many hands were at work editing, revising, and adding to the contents.

Further historical-literary research revealed that added to the words of Isaiah of Jerusalem, who lived in the eighth century B.C.E., were the teachings of an unknown author who lived in Babylon during the sixth century B.C.E.[3] This meant that Isaiah did not predict the release of Jews enslaved in Babylon two centuries after he lived. He did not receive divine insight that provided him with the name of the Persian deliverer—a king named Cyrus—long before the Persian kingdom came into being. That information was provided by someone who lived while Cyrus was alive and when the freeing of captive Jews was in progress (Isa. 45). Similar studies demonstrated that additions had been made to the work of other prophets, that David did not write the psalms attributed to him, that Solomon did not write Ecclesiastes or the Song of Songs, and so on.

What Christian and Jewish scholars have demonstrated beyond any doubt is that Tanak was a product of the temple. Its contents were either composed by priests and prophets and wise men associated with the temple or were given authority as divinely revealed documents by temple priests.[4]

I admit that I am making dramatic statements without providing evidence to prove my points. Fortunately, there are available in our libraries volume after volume of critical analysis by competent scholars, most of whom are Jewish or Christian. Their writings provide the needed supporting evidence.[5]

---

3. The eighth-century B.C.E. writings of Isaiah of Jerusalem are confined to the first thirty-nine chapters of the book. The writings from the sixth century and later appear in Isaiah 40-66.

4. Dever, "Archaeology and the Bible," 53, notes: "Ultimately, the Bible as we have it is almost entirely a product of the royal court and the priestly establishment in Jerusalem."

5. For example, Bernard Anderson, *Understanding the Old Testament* (Englewood Cliffs, NJ: 1986). For a sampling of more detailed studies, see Robert Alter and Frank Kermode, eds., *The Literary Guide to the Bible* (Cambridge, MA: Harvard University Press, 1987); Frank Moore Cross, *Canaanite Myth and Hebrew Epic: Essays in the History of the Religion of Israel* (Cambridge, MA: Harvard University Press, 1973); William H. Stiebing, Jr., *Out of the Desert? Archaeology and the Exodus/Conquest Narratives* (Buffalo, NY: Prometheus Books, 1989); Ernst Wurthwein, *The Text of the Old Testament: An Introduction to the Biblia Hebraica*, trans. Erroll F. Rhodes (Grand Rapids, MI: Eerdmans Publishing Co., 1979). Even conservative treatments admit pseudonymous authorship, later embellishment, and redaction. See, for

Both Near Eastern archaeology and comparative religion studies have contributed to biblical analysis. One of the best examples can be found in the creation narratives. For a long time readers of the Bible struggled over the fact that there appeared to be two different accounts of the creation in Genesis. In one story—which extends from Genesis 2:4b to the end of chapter 3—the reader is introduced to a lifeless world, where the only moisture came from a mist that dampened the soil and made it malleable.[6] Analysts attribute this account to a writer called "J."[7] Yahweh took the malleable clay (Hebrew: *adamah*, feminine) and formed a male figure. The clay was animated when, like an Arab midwife, Yahweh blew into the nostrils and caused the clay figure to breathe. Yahweh's next act was to plant a garden or an orchard, and the animated figure, now identified as a man (Hebrew: *adam*), was put in the garden to tend the plants.

Because the man was lonely, Yahweh once again took dampened earth to create a suitable companion. What he produced was an interminable collection of animals, birds, and insects which, like a proud artist, he presented, one by one, to the human for reaction. One by one they were named or given identities and rejected—camels and polar bears, lizards and hippopotami, mosquitoes and butterflies, apes and gorillas, penguins, ostriches, geese and pigeons—not one was acceptable as a companion.

Finally Yahweh put the man to sleep, removed a rib from his side, and from it fashioned a potential companion. The man's reaction was ecstasy: "At last!" he exclaimed, "this is it!" and so woman came into being.

Apparently the animals and humans lived amicably and were able to communicate. The snake, which was wiser and smarter than all

example, David Ewert, *From Ancient Tablets to Modern Translations: A General Introduction to the Bible* (Grand Rapids, MI: Zondervan Publishing House, 1983).

6. Gen. 2:10-14, which clearly interrupt the flow of the story, were added later by some unknown editor. There was no reference to "rivers" in the earlier version.

7. The source is called "J" because of the German spelling of the name of the Hebrew god "Yahweh" as "Jahveh."

other creatures (including the man), revealed to the woman one of Yahweh's secrets: the fruit of the tree of the knowledge of good and evil would not produce instantaneous death as Yahweh had claimed ("the day you eat, you die"), it would empower them with the capacity to make moral judgments and thereby elevate them above the simple animal realm into the category of human beings which was much closer to the status of deity (Gen. 3:4-5). The serpent spoke the truth: Yahweh had lied.[8]

When his deception was disclosed, Yahweh was angry. He realized that only immortality separated humans from becoming divine creatures, and because the wondrous tree of immortal life was also in his garden, he ejected the two humans (and apparently all of the animals) from the garden. To prevent reentry, he posted at the gateway cherubim and a flaming sword empowered to turn in any direction.

From that moment on, humans were to be on their own in a hostile environment. When they planted gardens, weeds vied with life-sustaining plants. They lived by the sweat of their brow—a concept that provides a biblical basis for the western work ethic. The harmonious relationship between animals and humans was broken forever because Yahweh killed animals and used their hides to make coverings for the couple.

The J creation account was composed as temple literature during the reign of King Solomon. Why? Because every temple in the various cultures of the Near Eastern world had its own creation myth to explain how their particular deity or deities created life, and to delineate the place and function of humans in the world. Like other Near Eastern creation accounts, the J myth taught that humans were

---

8. Deliberate deception by lying is not an uncommon motif in the early writings. Cain lied when asked where his brother Abel was (Gen. 4:9); Abram and Sarah lied about their marital relationship (Gen. 12:10-20; 20:1-8), as did Isaac regarding Rebekah (Gen. 26:6-11); Sarah lied when Yahweh accused her of laughing (Gen. 18:9-15); both Rebekah and Jacob lied to Jacob (Gen. 27); Laban deceived Jacob (Gen. 29:15-30); Rachel lied to her father Laban (Gen. 31:34-35) and so on. It seems that the most important moral requirement was not to be caught lying and, if caught, to justify the lie.

primarily created to be servants of the deity. So far as the ultimate meaning of human existence was concerned, J focused on agriculture and the struggle of human beings to produce food. Human beings were not immortal; they would return to the earth (*adamah*) from whence they came.

From excavations in Sumeria, archaeologists have recovered clay tablets that inform us that Sumerians, who existed millennia before the Hebrews, believed that in the beginning the earth was a desolate waste. Their gods shaped humans from clay to serve divine needs.[9] The same pattern appears in the Babylonian creation myth. A similar motif is found in the Egyptian story of the creation of humans from clay on a potter's wheel by the god Khnum. In other words, the biblical J account employed ideas that were present in surrounding cultures. The Hebrew story attributed creation to their god Yahweh and tied their myth to agricultural life in Canaan.

So far as the cherubim are concerned, they are not to be thought of as chubby figures of Renaissance art. They are like the Assyrian *kerubim*, monstrous winged animal creatures with human faces, crowns of horns, and bodies that combined the power of the lion and the bull. Such figures can be seen in the Assyrian section of the British Museum. When they were excavated, they were found to have been placed as protective figures at the entrances to palace precincts.

The other biblical creation myth, which opens the book of Genesis (1:1 to 2:4a), stands in stark contrast to the J account. This myth was composed between the sixth and fifth centuries and drew directly from the Babylonian creation account called *enuma elish*. *Enuma elish* first became known to the modern world when in 1876 a British scholar named George Smith translated it from clay tablets in the British Museum that had been recovered during excavations at Nineveh.[10]

---

9. For an extended discussion on the Near Eastern creation myths, see Gerald A. Larue, *Ancient Myth and Modern Life* (Long Beach: Centerline Press, 1988), chap. 2.

10. James B. Pritchard, ed., "The Creation Epic," *Ancient Near Eastern Texts Relating to the Old Testament*, trans. E. A. Speiser (Princeton, NJ: Princeton University Press, 1950), 60-72.

In this new Hebrew creation myth, the image of the god molding humans out of clay was abandoned. Now humans were created by God's "word." The order of creation in Genesis 1 follows that of the Babylonian account and introduces the notion of a primeval ocean in which the world exists. The world was thought of as a flat disc overarched by a hard firmament which kept out the waters above. The earth prevented the waters from below from surging up within the hemisphere. In contrast to the J story, in this new account birds, sea creatures, and animals are all created before human beings.

Apparently Jewish leaders held captive in Babylon found the Babylonian account to be more sophisticated than the earlier J version, but because the J story had been accorded authority in the temple, they did not discard it. They simply placed the new myth in front of the old one and let both stand.[11]

This revised biblical creation account, which scholars call "P" for "priest," borrowed motifs that were current in surrounding cultures. Creation by word had been attributed to the god Ptah of Egypt for centuries. The idea of primeval waters and a flat earth overarched by a solid heaven had been accepted for millennia in Egypt and Mesopotamia. The fact that two different creation myths could stand side by side is paralleled in Egypt where several authoritative creation myths existed simultaneously.

Perhaps one more example of the multiple authorship and of borrowing from other cultures will suffice.[12] Archaeological excavation has produced tablets providing the oldest known form of the Near Eastern flood story. In this third millennium B.C.E. Sumerian tale a priest-king named Ziusudra is the hero. From the fragmented text we learn that after the flood he offered animal sacrifices to the gods. A more complete flood myth was included in the Babylonian

---

11. See Alexander Heidel, *The Babylonian Genesis*, 2d ed. (Chicago: University of Chicago Press, 1951). See also Larue, *Ancient Myth*, 63a ff.

12. I choose this example deliberately because of the brouhaha that has occurred as a result of the hoax Sun International of Utah attempted to press on the public through their television film "The Amazing Discovery of Noah's Ark"—a discovery that was never made! See *Free Inquiry* 13 (Spring 1993); *Time*, 5 July 1993, 51.

legend of Gilgamesh, king of Uruk, who learned of the flood from an ancestor named Utnapishtim. It seems that Utnapishtim had been warned that the gods were going to destroy the world by flood. He was instructed to build an ark and to take aboard one pair of each living life form. After the flood, because he had saved the "seed of life," he was awarded immortality. Motifs in Utnapishtim's account of the flood are echoed in the biblical story. Utnapishtim sent out birds—in his story it was the raven that did not come back thus signaling that it was time to unload the ark. The ark was grounded on a mountain named Mount Nisir (Pir Omar Gudun). Upon landing, Utnapishtim offered sacrifices to the gods.

The Gilgamesh epic circulated for centuries in the Near East and was known in Palestine before the coming of the Hebrews.[13]

Like Utnapishtim, Noah was warned of the impending flood, told to build an ark and bring aboard pairs of all living creatures. Like Utnapishtim, Noah's boat landed on a mountain ("amidst the mountains of Ararat," not on Mount Ararat). Like Utnapishtim Noah sent out birds and like the Babylonian hero Noah offered sacrifice after exiting the ark.

During the fifth century priestly writers overwrote the earlier J flood account. In the J story, Noah took on board seven pair of those animals which, according to Hebrew law, were considered to be ritually clean, but only one pair of unclean animals. There was good reason for this difference in numbers. At the end of the J story, Noah, like Utnapishtim, offered animal sacrifice to Yahweh. If only one pair of each had been taken aboard, all clean animals would have perished.

Priestly writers also argued that from the time of creation up to the post-flood era, humans were vegetarians. It was only after the flood that humans could eat animals and birds and fish (Gen. 9:1-4). Further, because priestly writers were enamored of the idea of covenants between god and people, they included a covenant agree-

---

13. D. J. Wiseman, *Illustrations From Biblical Archaeology* (Grand Rapids, MI: W. B. Eerdmans, 1958), 13, notes that a fragment of the Gilgamesh Epic was found in the fourteenth-century B.C.E. level in the excavation at Megiddo.

ment whereby god promised to never again destroy life on earth by flood. To remind himself of his promise not to flood the earth again, the deity placed the rainbow in the sky (Gen. 9:13-16).

Archaeological research has provided some evidence that enhances our understanding of Near Eastern flood mythology. There is clear evidence that in Mesopotamia, the Tigris and Euphrates rivers have, from time to time, overflowed their banks and inundated nearby communities. For example, Sir Leonard Woolley in his excavations of ancient al Ubaid found deep levels of river silt covering habitation, indicating that the site had been completely covered by water. Above the silt levels community living began again.[14] It is possible that the flood myth developed out of such recurring flood experiences. Such a myth would not normally develop in Israel where the only river, the Jordan, flows below sea level. Obviously the Hebrew tale is borrowed.[15]

Finally, I would like to suggest that one does not need to be a biblical scholar, an expert in comparative religions, or an archaeologist to become aware of discrepancies in the Bible. One need only use common sense and employ a critical eye. The secularist is able to approach the Bible with common sense partly because he or she does not read through the eyes of faith seeking spiritual guidance or insight. The secularist reads because the magnificent prose and poetry of Tanak has contributed metaphors to our language and has impacted in important ways the arts, societal attitudes, and conduct.

---

14. L. Woolley, *Ur of the Chaldees* (Harmondsworth, Middlesex, Eng.: Penguin Books, 1950), chap. 1; A. Parrot, *The Flood and Noah's Ark*, trans. E. Hudson (New York: Philosophical Library, 1955), 13ff.

15. Other borrowings include the Hebrew temple modelled on Canaanite temples; the language of many of the psalms which echoes the ritual language of ancient Canaanite religion recorded on clay tablets from the Ras es-Shamra excavations; a fourteenth-century Egyptian hymn to the sun-god Aton (cf. Psalms 114); Proverbs 22:17-24:22 attributed to Solomon but borrowed from the wisdom of Amen-em-opet of Egypt; the imagery of the suffering servant in Isaiah 52:13-53:12 formulated from a ceremony of ritual cleansing that was part of the Babylonian Akitu festival; and the apocalyptic eschatology of the book of Daniel drawn from end-of-the-age imagery of Zoroastrian religion.

Like the religious scholar, the secularist asks: Where did this literature come from? Who wrote it? When? Why? But then adds: Why do
so many people accept it literally and uncritically or believe it to be
divinely revealed? And, does it make sense?

For the secularist reader, using the common sense approach, the
creation myth in Genesis 1 makes no sense. The secularist asks: How
can there be three days of day and night before the sun is created on
the fourth day? The answer from scholars is: That is the way the
account read in the Babylonian myth from which the Hebrews
borrowed the pattern. To understand it we have to ask how the
Babylonians reached such a conclusion—but no one seems to care
much about what the Babylonians thought.

In the J creation myth, the formation of man, then animals, and
then woman makes no sense in terms of the evolution of species. The
idea that woman was formed from man may imply a romantic reality
suggesting that many of us males feel incomplete until we have found
our missing rib, but this is not scientific reality.

The flood story makes no sense. The idea that the earth is a flat
disc and that earth and sky meet at the horizon is an optical illusion.
There is no firmament above keeping out waters above, nor are there
windows in the sky for the deity to open and cause a flood. There
never was a worldwide flood that covered Mount Everest. Noah's
wooden boat, which was three times larger than any wooden craft
ever built and which was one-and-a-half times the length of a modern
football field, would have broken apart—wood is not strong enough
to build such a huge sea-going vessel.

The gathering of animals is also nonsense. First, Noah's boat
would never hold all of the species—even Sir Walter Raleigh realized
that back in the seventeenth century when he wrote his two-volume
History of the World. Moreover, the idea of polar bears and penguins,
American buffalo and llamas, kangaroos from Australia—none of
which were known to the ancients—journeying all the way to Palestine
is fantasy. The idea of a rainbowless antedeluvian sky makes no sense
since it suggests that the laws of refraction were different before the
flood than after.[16]

16. And, I might add, that despite the claim made in the Sun

Secularists find it difficult to grasp that Joshua could have made the sun stand still by holding up his arms, that more than a million Hebrews could have wandered for forty years in the Sinai and survived primarily on manna (pea-sized granules produced on tamarisk bushes one month each year), or that Joshua and his priests blowing on ram's horns or shofars could have caused the huge walls of Jericho to collapse. Indeed, those walls were collapsed by earthquake and the city abandoned more than a century before the coming of the Hebrews.

What we learn from an open-minded inquiry into biblical literature is that these writings, like all other writings, reflect the time in which they were produced. In biblical times the world was believed to be inhabited by spirits or powers both benevolent (angelic) and malevolent (demonic). The writings are considered to be holy or divinely revealed because temple priests who lived 2,000-3,000 years ago said they were. When we recognize that biblical literature is simply *literature*, we are able to recognize and separate myth from court history, legend from fable, fantasy thinking from reality, and so forth. We are also able to recognize that the attitudes and viewpoints presented in these writings represent what men and women once believed.

Biblical attitudes toward women and homosexuals represent the narrow, patriarchal thinking of the people in those ancient times. Unfortunately, by giving these time-limited writings divine authority, ancient bigotry and discrimination continue to function in our own times, thereby limiting the freedom, rights, creativity, and potentials of women and homosexuals.

So long as these writings are accorded divine authority, students in public schools will be handicapped by those who insist that non-scientific biblical creationism be given scientific status in school curricula. Already their contentiousness has resulted in a tendency to avoid the use of the scientific term "evolution" in texts and teaching. Like women and homosexuals, native American Indians,

---

production, there is no destructive flood myth found in ancient Egyptian literature, nor are they accurate when they state that flood stories "worldwide" accord with the biblical account.

African Americans, Asian Americans, and others will be evaluated, stigmatized, and socially segregated on the basis of biblical passages. Their efforts to experience full recognition as human beings and as Americans will be thwarted and frustrated.

Our intent as rational investigators of biblical literature is not to offend "true believers"; our concern is to present the best findings of critical scholarship. As educators, and in keeping with the highest aims of our profession, we seek to free students from whatever tends to limit their thinking and spirit of open inquiry in the hope that we make some contribution toward lifting human life a bit closer to its highest potential. Unexamined ideas, whether assumptions or beliefs, confine the spirit and mind.

I do not deny that many kind and gracious acts and programs have been motivated by biblical teachings and commandments. I find no fault with those who reach out to others in need because they are told that this is what their deity requires of them or because they believe they will be judged in an afterlife on the basis of obedience to such commands. Helping others is always honorable, noble, and in accord with the highest humanistic ideals.

When secularists make humanistic and humanitarian outreaches, they do not act because they are commanded or required to do so by religious scriptures. Humanists respond to need, to hurt, to sorrow out of compassion, caring, love, and responsibility for others—feelings that well up from within the human psyche. We are free spirits who seek to respond to our highest dreams and achieve our noblest potentials, not because we are told we must, but because we care and because we freely choose to act on the basis of our own caring. Such choice places us in control of our own destinies and helps us to become aware of our human potential for making moral and ethical judgments.

If Jews, Christians, and Mormons have a message for this troubled world, so do secular humanists. Our message does not come from writings assumed to be sacred. We are concerned with life-giving freedom, with life-sustaining power, with exploration of the human potentials for peace and goodwill and harmony, with fulfillment of the highest human ideals for justice, truth, beauty, and love, in all the changing contexts of life and society. We are eager to expand the horizons of human learning and human understanding and our motivation comes from within, from those deep well-springs of love and caring. Therefore, when we approach authoritative scripture, whether it be the Bible or the Book of Mormon, we do not abandon critical faculties. We bring to our examination the best analytical tools of our professions whether they be literary and historical analysis, or the fruits of archaeological research and studies in comparative religion, or simply good old common sense. Our commitment is not only to call forth the caring and feeling and responding human being, but also to empower the rational human being.

4.
Freedom of Conscience: Individual Right or Social Responsibility?

L. Jackson Newell

Levi Zendt, a central figure in James Michener's novel *Centennial*, was raised in a small Amish town in Pennsylvania. He chafed under the pious expectation of his elders, rebelled against the orthodoxy they pressed on him, and was shunned as a teenager for his unwillingness to do what they wished him to do. With the aid of an understanding grandmother and a few dollars from her apron pocket, Zendt rode out of town stopping only at the village orphanage to whisk away Elly, the love of his young life. The two of them followed the trail of westering Americans in the early 1840s, making their way to St. Louis behind their prancing steeds, but trading them there for two trusty oxen that would eat less and pull harder on the long overland trail to Colorado.

Young Levi and Elly resolved to homestead on the edge of the prairie in the evening shadow of the Rocky Mountains. She died shortly from a rattlesnake bite, but the story traces Levi's long life on the Colorado frontier. In Michener's tale, Levi becomes an irrepressible force for education, civilization, and peace. As the area he homesteaded becomes a village, and then a town, and finally a small city, Levi raises his voice for schools, builds libraries, and stands for justice in a wild land. He seeks to understand, and then to reconcile, the bitter differences in perspective taken by cattle ranchers and sheepherders, by Scottish and German settlers and Arapaho and Shoshone Indians. Levi Zendt is full of compassion for all who are

31

treated shabbily by the severe weather and harsh culture of his time and place.

In his later years, Levi makes a pilgrimage to Lancaster County, Pennsylvania, and the village of his birth. There he begins to see what he had not consciously realized until that time. Although he had foregone the *trappings* of the religion of his youth—the forms of Amish worship—his life had been a near-perfect expression of the essential values he had been taught as a boy. I might say, though Michener wouldn't have put these words in Levi's mouth, that Levi had done what the elders of his youth had dared only to preach.

An intriguing question for all of us engaged in the present humanist-Mormon dialogue is whether Levi Zendt was a Christian or a humanist—or whether, in fact, such labels have any meaning. In one fashion or another, I've asked over a generation of university students to ponder this question. Nearing ninety years of age, Mormon academic and author Lowell Bennion captured the essence of this quintessential dilemma with the simple stroke of an artist: "If you doubt God," he recently said in an interview, "I hope you will not doubt what God stands for—truth and justice and mercy."

My topic is freedom of conscience and, with proper respect for Webster, I define freedom of conscience as the quality of living consciously and consistently within the framework of one's highest ideals. Freedom of conscience is the freedom beyond all freedoms, the ultimate freedom. Americans, more than most peoples, assume that freedom is measured by the number of options open to an individual at any moment. We have missed the point. Freedom is the ecstacy we experience when, over the long haul, we achieve the noblest aspirations we have carried in our hearts and minds.

Speaking and acting in accordance with our conscience hardly banishes pain or sorrow from our lives, but it certainly does spare us regret, remorse, and shame. "I have been to the mountaintop and I have seen the promised land," Martin Luther King, Jr., proclaimed shortly before his assassination, "and I don't fear any man anymore." Be we believer or skeptic, whatever words we use to describe the rare but exquisite confluence of the conscious self and the universe, we know it as liberty and feel it as joy.

Mortimer Adler, among others, has written about great ideas that have defined civilizations (*Six Great Ideas* [New York: Collier, 1981]).

Such ideas are the substance of conscience, the touchstones of ethical lives. I am talking here about the essential values of world cultures that have stood out above all others. I call these "enduring ideas" because no individual, nor any society, can exist one day without encountering, consciously or unconsciously, the need to confront and make decisions about these human values.

From the ancient Greeks, we draw three: goodness, truth, and beauty. From the European enlightenment, three more: liberty, justice, and equality. From most of the great religions of the world, I think we must add three more: peace, mercy and love.

Now the Greeks had no corner on goodness, beauty, and truth, or even on the articulation of those values, and the same is true of the intellectual leaders of the Enlightenment. But these were two times and places in history where civilization seemed particularly adept at stating ideals and struggling to realize them in human institutions and behavior. In the same way, the major religions of the world have been porters of the venerable and humanizing concepts of love, mercy and peace.

Most of the struggles in our society and around the globe today can be seen as quests to reconcile the competing demands of two or more of these nine enduring ideas. Courts wrestle with justice and mercy, Congress with liberty and equality, religions with love and truth, and perennial negotiators in the Middle East with peace and justice. To understand these ideas, to see them more consciously at play in our own hearts and in life around us, is to hold out the possibility of gathering wisdom in any human soul.

Many words have been spent, ink spilled, and good will squandered over the clash of some of these values in the institutional life of the Church of Jesus Christ of Latter-day Saints. By the summer of 1993 the Mormon church had become so immersed in its struggle to control free expression among its membership that it began to appear that nothing mattered as much as obedience and orthodoxy. As church "disciplinary councils" were urged into action, and some members' lives were tragically disrupted, particularly the "September Six," the intellectual, feminist, and homosexual communities engaged the conflict with such zeal that it bordered on obsession.

As important as these matters are, and continue to be, it is vital that we think beyond them, beyond free inquiry alone. Freedom of conscience and free expression are not ends in themselves, but means for the liberation of the human spirit. They are qualities of mind that enable us to address courageously the great issues of our time. Like a new baseball mitt, freedom of conscience has a wonderful aroma, but it is of little value until you break it in . . . and take the field.

My personal list of the major issues on the field of human affairs in our era is a long one, but I want to present what I regard as the most crucial three. At the top of my list I place biological survival. Threats to the global ecosystem are now so pervasive and severe that the vast majority of us—including public officials, religious leaders, and academics—will do anything to shield ourselves from the awful reality. All the while, we are sucking the earthly battery dry of its reserve of carbon energy, stripping away that precious six-inch layer of top soil on which production of almost all our food and fiber depends, poisoning our water, and despoiling the blanket of air without which we cannot breathe.

There are many reasons for the eco-crisis, but the explosion of the world's population during the last several hundred years overwhelms all the others. The rise of science and the use of technology are both a cause and an effect of the Malthusian curve. We have already exceeded the earth's carrying capacity for human beings, in the judgment of many scientists, with or without technological advances and agricultural miracles.

The control of population growth, even the reduction of the human population by drastically reducing birth rates in North America (where each child consumes far more of the earth's resources than anywhere else) and worldwide, is the single most important step that we can take to assure survival—not just for the human species, but perhaps for all higher animal life on this planet.

The second most grave problem facing our society and the larger world today is the disintegration of viable family units. I refer not to *the* family unit, but *any* family unit or set of family units that can exist together and be pervasive enough to assure the loving and healthy rearing of children everywhere. The number of unloved and unwanted children today is appalling, and also relates to the above-mentioned problem of excessive population growth. When I say "unwanted," I speak not only of unexpected pregnancies but more importantly of children who are *de facto* orphaned by parents who simply decide, somewhere along the line, that they no longer wish to accept the responsibility to rear them. This problem is epidemic, striking families across the socio-economic spectrum and children of all ages and races.

The traditional family has almost vanished as a result of twentieth-century changes in economics, demographics, science, and technology. As Rollo May has said, "We are living at a time when one age is dying and the new age is not yet born" (*The Courage to Create* [New York: Bantam Books, 1975], 1). At any moment in history, however, we are only one generation away from barbarism—because even that is a generous estimate of the time we have to introduce each newborn child to the enduring ideas that hold civilizations together, and to inspire each child with a sense of safety and duty and responsibility. Nobody can reasonably believe that we're making headway on this front.

The answer, of course, is not to turn back the clock and rediscover the nuclear or "traditional" family. It can't be done, not as a universal institution or anything close to it. In cases where such families do survive and flourish, at least those where gender equality is highly valued, it can be a source of great strength for all its members, and for society. But this experience is no longer common.

Most children in the ghettos of Los Angeles, Rio, or Hong Kong—and probably even Salt Lake City—are now living without their two biological parents, and many are out of contact even with one. The latest demographic studies suggest that less than half of the children in the United States today live with both of their biological parents, and many are experiencing the breakup of a series of short-term "family units" before reaching adulthood (see Barbara Dafoe Whitehead, "Dan Quayle Was Right," *Atlantic Monthly*, Apr. 1993).

My third-ranking problem which warrants our action is the maldistribution of wealth and privilege within our society—and within and among every society around the world. Every year more mansions creep up the mountain slopes ringing Salt Lake Valley and every year more homeless and hungry men, women, and children huddle in Pioneer Park and beg along our main streets. Our local economy, like the world economy, is geared to capitalize upon and reward the advantages of formal education and training. As the work of the world takes place increasingly in huge institutions (or is regulated by huge institutions), there is not so wide a berth as there once was for the variety of people, personalities and motivations that impel us to work and to give our energies and talents for the common good. Homelessness and hunger, here and abroad, are not simply problems of shortages, or even of lacking skills; they are also problems of human motivation.

Like the first two problems, then, the maldistribution of wealth is one that has highly complex causes and severe consequences. War and revolution are the inevitable outcomes of stark differences in the human condition, and reform has always been the best antidote to revolution. The twentieth century has seen a variety of radical and even bizarre experiments to address the disparities between rich and poor, and between the powerful and powerless. Most have collapsed in tragic and bloody heaps. Reform is almost always the more humane road to lasting, positive change.

In searching for Mormon and humanist responses to my list of the three most pressing global problems, I place my hope for the resolutions in three institutions: education, democracy, and a regulated market economy. In an increasingly technological world economy, the importance of education appears self evident. The work of the world is no longer accomplished by muscle power. Happily, it is also true worldwide that the higher the level of education the lower the birth rate. Significantly, education is also essential to the full functioning of the other two institutions—democracy and a regulated market economy.

As Thomas Jefferson perceived so clearly 200 years ago, free institutions cannot flourish or even survive without an educated citizenry. Democracy can't work without education, real education of the type we call liberal. And regulated capitalism can exist only with wise and courageous public officials and politicians.

As the former Soviet Union and its satellite states revealed, when indoctrination replaces education the result is a dependent citizenry—politically, economically, and morally. And where training is thought to suffice instead of education, free institutions and responsible economic production will not be found.

Vigorous, free, and liberal education is where I put my faith and where I have been fortunate to put my energies throughout my career. I'm more convinced than ever that those of us who devote our lives to the education of children and adults are investing our energies at one of the most crucial points in the complex web of human experience today.

Robust democratic institutions offer hope for responding to the ecological disaster, the imperiled notion of family (in any form), and the disparity between rich and poor. Elected officials *must* pay attention to the interests of the poor, so long as the franchise is universal. By the same token, elected officials must respond to the disintegration of families and the moral, physical, and spiritual suffering of children.

Recent assessments of environmental damage in the former Soviet Union and Warsaw Pact nations make it clear that governments that are not responsible to the people are not responsible to the earth or to other creatures that inhabit it. The worst environmental disasters in history were caused and covered up by authoritarian regimes.

Unquestionably, market economics has been the source of many of the worst assaults on the global environment, but, paradoxically, modern capitalism is our best hope for responding to these disasters. Given the number of people who are swarming around this earth today, it is clear that without responsible economic development we will burn every twig, eat every fruit, and despoil every spring with our own excretion. Responsible free market economics, made possible by liberal education, in the context of a sturdy democratic political system, not only offers the best hope of reducing family size and world population, but also of raising environmental consciousness and responsibility. We must work to improve these institutions, and we should turn our attention increasingly to the problems that matter most. We must find some way to get beyond the obsession with church policies and politics in Utah and beyond the humanist-religionist impasse in the larger American society.

One way we might do this is by recognizing the contributions that can be made to these more fundamental problems by both Mormons and humanists. Having spent a good portion of my life as a Mormon outside of Utah, I have seen the positive effects on people who embrace the faith and the doctrine of the LDS church. I believe there is ample evidence that interest and pursuit of education increases dramatically with membership in the Mormon church, and I would wager that participation in the political process, and even economic independence (and the capacity to contribute more than one gives to the economy), also increase. However, one must get outside of Utah to see this clearly.

On the other hand, I can't give the LDS church high marks in other areas. It can cause people to be dangerously dependent on leaders rather than to think for themselves. It also provides encouragement and rationale for extremely large families. In the areas where it is dominant, the conservative political weight of Mormon culture augers against the exploration of almost all solutions to poverty, illiteracy, and the troubled family—except those prescribed by Mormon leaders.

Here is where humanists make one of their crucial contributions. One of the difficulties of the Mormon world view is the belief that a divine plan exists which assures that everything will work out just fine in the end. Don't worry about the survival of civilization or of life on earth, the Millennium will come, and must come, anyway. Don't worry about overpopulation, we have been instructed to populate and replenish the earth and bring those spirits down from heaven.

A humanist perspective is much more realistic about our *human* responsibility to respond to contemporary problems. We need the desperately sober and highly rational world view of humanism, and we need the sense of responsibility that comes with it. I do not believe we are going to be rescued by miracles, be they technological or divine. But we might do much to rescue ourselves through courage, good sense and hard work.

Both Mormonism and humanism provide a healthy response to the pervasive cynicism that engulfs the contemporary world. Both give me good reason to believe that it matters greatly what *I* do. Both call you and me to consider the interests of those far away from us in time and place, and both, at least at their best, demand a high degree of commitment to common endeavors. I for one refuse to dichotomize Mormonism and humanism, or Christianity and humanism, or to pit them against one another. I regard myself as a Christian humanist—rather than a secular humanist—acknowledging that the broad ethics of Jesus, as distinct from the institutional church, have a powerful claim on my philosophy and actions.

I owe a personal and intellectual debt to both Mormonism and humanism. Certainly, I understand the singular enduring ideas far better because I have seen them through both of these lenses. Taking a cue from the story of Levi Zendt, and from the wisdom of Lowell Bennion, I hope we can all—skeptics and believers—recommit ourselves to the highest and most enduring ideals of human civilizations.

There is no greater hope for humanity, nor any greater threat to tyranny and injustice, than a free and responsible conscience, coupled with the courage and will to act. The celebration of our freedom must be dwarfed by, and given meaning through, the dedication of our energies to the relief of suffering and the advance of human dignity worldwide.

Part II
Academic Freedom

5.
Academic Freedom at Brigham Young University: Free Inquiry in Religious Context

Allen Dale Roberts

Nestled at the foot of the rugged Wasatch Mountains, Brigham Young University, with more than 30,000 students, is well-known as the nation's largest religiously-sponsored private university. With 1,500 full-time faculty in ten colleges and two professional schools, BYU offers 130 undergraduate programs and fifty-seven graduate departments, as well as a law school and graduate school of management.

The student body is composed of about 10,000 Utah students, 18,000 from other states and 2,000 from foreign countries. About 49 percent are women and 51 percent are men; 25 percent are married and 40 percent have served Mormon missions. The student body gets increasingly bright, with entering freshmen in 1989 averaging 24.7 on ACTs (compared with a national average of 18.6), and an average high school GPA of 3.43. These are the highest figures for any university in Utah, and they climb higher each year.

The faculty is well-trained and highly regarded in many departments. Most are Mormon and combine teaching responsibilities with extensive church and community service. BYU's campus is well-maintained, and its physical facilities and equipment are, in many instances, state-of-the-art. Anyone visiting the campus cannot help but be impressed with the freshly washed appearance of the grounds, buildings, faculty, and students.

But close observers also find that something is wrong with this picture. It is incomplete and more than a little out of focus. One would expect, with all of its assets, that BYU would be one of the leading institutions of higher education in the country, if not the world. But despite its many advantages, BYU is not renowned for academic excellence (in the last independent rating of universities I read, BYU was not mentioned as being highly ranked in any of its departments). And it is by no means an unrelated development that the campus is beset with serious difficulties connected to its restrictive policies and limitation of freedom.

Owned, sponsored, paid for, and entirely governed by leaders of the Church of Jesus Christ of Latter-day Saints, BYU is, by its own design and admission, first and foremost a church institution and secondarily a school. Working under the burden of institutionally-imposed and severely limiting definitions of truth and intellectual freedom, both the university's academic freedom and academic competence are increasingly called into question. Because of its nearly total dependence on the LDS church, BYU administrators, faculty, and students alike are vulnerable to losses in scholastic integrity and freedom at the hand of an authoritarian, manipulative, and anti-intellectual church.

Controlled closely by a board of trustees composed entirely of church leaders, the university must meet the expectations and requirements imposed by trustees. The trustees have made it clear, as evident in a 1993 document justifying the limitation of academic freedom as a school policy, that this is a university with an unusual mission. In a speech which may have caused some internal hemorrhaging among administrators and fund-raisers, trustee Boyd K. Packer invited faculty members and students who value academic freedom to leave BYU and seek the freedom they desire at one of the country's other 3,500 colleges and universities. As we examine trustee attitudes to higher education, we can get a better picture of why academic freedom is a virtual impossibility at BYU.

At this point perhaps we should ask, What is a university? Clearly, this simple question does not lend itself to a single, easy answer. I have heard some facile responses and have myself provided reductionist summaries: an educational institution in which all propositions may be discussed freely and openly. While I may hold this to be a goal worthy of universities, it reflects neither the history nor the diversity of contemporary campuses.

From the inception of the college and university concept in medieval Europe until the late nineteenth and early twentieth centuries, most universities were founded and operated by churches. Their guiding principles were consistent with those espoused by BYU today. They were committed to providing the best available knowledge, both religious and secular, and in many instances, no distinction was made between the two. In fact, throughout most ages of civilization, academic inquiry was a manifestation of religious curiosity.

According to Charles W. Anderson in his book, *Prescribing the Life of the Mind*, both science and philosophy were always regarded as sacred vocations: "This was simply assumed at Athens, at Alexandria, throughout the Middle Ages, and by most of the great thinkers of the high Enlightenment. Our era is startlingly difficult in this regard. Today it is widely assumed that science and religion are not only distinct but antagonistic."

In the rationalist, post-enlightenment world, however, a new concept emerged, as described in theologian Cardinal John Henry Newman's influential *Idea of a University*, and refined many times since, most recently by Jaroslav Pelikan in his *The Idea of the University: A Reexamination*. A professor of religious studies at Yale University, Pelikan stresses the virtues of "free inquiry, scholarly honesty, civility in discourse, toleration of diverse beliefs and values, and trust in rationality and public verifiability."

In my own five-year experience as a BYU student and recent observations of the school, it seems to me that BYU scores low marks in attaining most of these virtues. This is in large part because it continues to pursue the ecclesiastical model of a university.

The recent *Encyclopedia of Mormonism* explains BYU's mission as, in part, "to assist individuals in their quest for perfection and eternal life," and to "study . . . all truth . . . especially . . . the saving truths of the gospel of Jesus Christ." As Dallin Oaks expressed during his inauguration as BYU president, "Our reason for *being* is to be a university. But our *reason* for being a university is to encourage and prepare young men and women to rise to their full potential as sons and daughters of God."

For Mormons, this idea of combining spiritual and temporal learning had its origins with Joseph Smith, who taught that there is no difference between the two types of knowledge. A self-taught man with a voracious appetite for learning, Smith also wrote,

> Teach ye diligently and my grace shall attend you, that you may be instructed more perfectly in . . . things both in the heaven and in the earth, and under the earth; things which must shortly come to pass . . . a knowledge also of countries and kingdoms . . . Seek learning out of the best books words of wisdom . . . seek learning, even by study and also by faith.

Church leaders and administrators assert that church sponsorship of BYU is its greatest strength. Says academic vice-president Bruce Hafen in his color metaphor describing the school's dual role, the blue world of the church "enables greater, not lesser educational perfection than the red [higher education] world knows."

In the annual president's address in August 1993, Rex Lee vowed that BYU will not lose sight of its commitment to "the ideal of a church university." He reiterated that the school would not follow the course of most other universities which "abandon their spiritual component and concentrate solely on the academic." Lee did not speak of balance, or of the limitations of such an attitude. Like LDS apostle Joseph Fielding Smith and others, the view is that religious considerations are superior to the aims of scholarship.

The best evidence is that the board of trustees is almost entirely composed of "prophets, seers and revelators," while "deeply committed members of the LDS church dominate the faculty." Clearly there is no attempt to have balanced representation at any level. Still, Lee and Hafen have expressed a commitment to excellence in both scholarship and faith. "This is our distinction," said Lee.

The public relations ingenuity of this kind of pronouncement is apparent, but is it a real distinction or a mirage? I believe that the school's two goals are mutually unobtainable because in an institution where religion demands dominance and is suspicious of secular knowledge, and where suppression of academic freedom is an openly stated policy, academic excellence is an impossibility. In this regard,

I find myself in agreement with humanist writer Vern Bullough who says, "Religious orthodoxy and the intellectual freedom necessary for higher education are simply contradictory components."

So the old problem surfaces. The church's controlling leaders do not believe in learning, knowledge, and truth for their own sakes. Instead, their epistemology is of the narrowest type. Whatever current leaders teach is true, no matter how illogical, unwise, unverifiable, or contradictory with past revealed truth. Anything different is untrue, no matter how logical or verifiable.

All of the classic theories of determining truth—by correspondence, coherence, and so forth—are invalid in Mormon epistemology. This ability to discard all truths in conflict with Mormon teachings is *the* distinctive characteristic of BYU and Mormonism.

How does this utilitarian view of truth affect teachers and students at BYU? Some seem untouched, especially those who are unquestioning or who study in technical fields. But others feel the conflict sharply. They know that there are vast numbers of ideas and issues which can never be discussed freely in the classroom. This limiting condition has its roots in a long unresolved Mormon conflict between the nature and role of knowledge.

In the preface to his 1908 book, *Joseph Smith as Scientist*, LDS apostle and Harvard Ph.D. John A. Widtsoe wrote, "In the life of every person who receives a higher education in or out of schools there is a time when there seems to be opposition between science and religion; between man-made and God-made knowledge. The struggle for reconciliation between the contending forces is not an easy one." He finds this ultimately unnecessary because, he says, "there is no real difference between science and religion." In another publication, *Centennial Tracts*, he espoused his belief that the gospel of Jesus Christ "comprehends all truth, whether of science, philosophy or religion. It includes, harmonizes, and moulds into one system, the truth of every cult, creed, sect or uplifting agency. It has courage to accept and teach and defend truth."

There are problems with this idea. If science proves that homosexuality, for example, is a genetic endowment rather than a learned behavior, will the Mormon church change its position on the subject? The same could be asked of organic evolution as well as various disciplines in the social sciences. The church has not entirely abandoned other disproven teachings. Would Mormonism be willing to accept a role of following the lead of science? I think not. Mormonism sees itself as leading out, not reacting, in the quest for knowledge.

Widtsoe elaborates on his earlier idea: "The great, fundamental laws of the Universe are foundation stones in religion as well as in science. The principle that matter is indestructible belongs as much to theology as to geology. The theology which rests upon the few basic laws of nature is unshakable, and the great theology of the future will be such a one." Widtsoe seems to envision a religion which progresses in part through accepting and integrating the advances of science and other reliable, worldly knowledge. As he saw it,

> "Mormonism" teaches and has taught from the beginning that all knowledge must be included in true theology. Because of its comprehensive philosophy, "Mormonism" will survive all religious disturbances and become the system of religious faith which all men may accept without yielding the least part of knowledge of nature as discovered in laboratories or in the fields.

Widtsoe's belief in Mormon philosophy as the eventual embodiment of "completely unified knowledge" might be expected from a rationalist/scientist, but even though a committee appointed by the First Presidency to read and critique his manuscript approved its publication, we can now see that his views were not those of the church, then or now.

One member of the manuscript review committee, Joseph Fielding Smith, later published his own much longer and more popular book, *Man: His Origin and Destiny*, in 1954, just after Widtsoe died. Smith held a very different view of science and its relation to religion. To get to the gist of his position, we need only read the subheadings under the word "science" in his index:

> Science, false teaching of
> Science, revelation superior to
> Scientific investigation, cannot demonstrate the resurrection
> Scientists, claim the Bible as myth
> Scientists, faith in scripture weakened by
> Scientists, false concepts of God of
> Scientists, reject fall and atonement

Scientists, revelations attacked by

Scientists will formulate false theories as long as they ignore the Divine Creator

Clearly Smith, who would later become president of the LDS church, did not share Widtsoe's view of the harmony of science and religion. Instead, he saw them as irreconcilable opponents. Moreover, all kinds of knowledge for him were not valid or coequal. Religious knowledge, or particularly, revealed Mormon knowledge, was "superior" to any other kind.

Although the battle over these two competing positions may have been fought to a draw during the lifetimes of scientists and rationalists such as Widtsoe, Joseph Merrill, and Brigham H. Roberts, it was Joseph Fielding Smith's theory of hierarchical knowledge that won the war and persists to this day.

When Smith asserted that "Revelation is superior to science," he had no difficulty in telling us which worldly knowledge was false. For example: "the most pernicious doctrine ever entering the mind of man [is] the theory that man evolved from lower forms of life," a teaching he believed originated in the devil and spread through his unwitting servants, "Darwin, Wallace and others."

Smith believed in the supremacy of scripture—Mormon scripture—literally interpreted, over any other kind of document, evidence, or knowledge. And of course his interpretation and those of other Mormon prophets were especially superior. This religio-centric attitude is not unique to Mormons, but we are singular in reducing to second-class or even heretical status any knowledge not held to have been "revealed."

Current church president Ezra Taft Benson, born at the end of the nineteenth century, has compounded the problem. In his 1980 speech, "Fourteen Fundamentals in Following the Prophet," delivered at BYU, then-apostle Benson identified the "grand key" for saving human souls—"Follow the Prophet." Consider the ramifications for academic freedom. Listen to the tone as well as the content (capitalization in original):

First: The Prophet is the Only Man Who Speaks for The Lord in Everything.
Second: The Living Prophet is More Vital to Us Than The

Standard Works (Mormon scriptures).

Third: The Living Prophet is More Important to Us Than a Dead Prophet.

Fourth: The Prophet Will Never Lead the Church Astray.

Fifth: The Prophet is Not Required to Have Any Particular Early Training or Credentials to Speak on Any Subject or Act on Any Matter at Any Time.

Eighth: The Prophet is Not Limited by Man's Reasoning.

Ninth: The Prophet can Receive Revelation on Any Matter—Temporal or Spiritual.

Tenth: The Prophet May be Involved in Civic Matters.

Eleventh: The Two Groups Who Have the Greatest Difficulty in Following the Prophet are the Proud Who Are Learned and the Proud Who are Rich.

Twelve: The Prophet Will Not Necessarily be Popular with the World or the Worldly.

Fourteen: The Prophet and the Presidency—The Living Prophet and the First Presidency—Follow Them and Be Blessed—Reject Them and Suffer.

Just three months after Benson's speech, another highly influential apostle, Bruce R. McConkie, followed up with his talk, "Seven Deadly Heresies," also delivered to BYU students. The controversial talk listed among the heresies the idea that "God is progressing in knowledge and is learning new truths," and the belief that "revealed religion and organic evolution can be harmonized." Still, McConkie could claim that "All truth is in agreement, and true religion and true science bear the same witness; indeed, true science is part of religion." This sounds like vintage Widtsoe. McConkie could say this, I believe, because he felt that in the end, scientific findings would support rather than contradict religious teachings.

The religious beliefs, pronouncements, and practices of Mormon leaders imperil academic excellence at BYU. Here are some of the difficulties I see, moving categorically from ideological issues pervasive churchwide to considerations that bear directly on the educational enterprise.

Mormonism suffers from an epistemological eliteness which bodes ill for free inquiry. Leaders hold a hierarchical view of knowledge in which the most important knowledge comes only to the few highest-ranking church leaders. While all members are urged to study and search for truth, LDS-sanctioned "truths" are never accepted solely on the basis of their own weight or merit. This reality has a chilling effect on the search for answers by those not high in ecclesiastical position.

Moreover, the truthfulness of all propositions is based on who said them and when. Recall that Ezra Taft Benson said that the statement of a living prophet supersedes the earlier statements of a dead prophet, including, presumably, Abraham, Moses, Jesus, or Joseph Smith. Those of you familiar with Benson's extremely conservative writings and teachings, especially those delivered in the 1950s and 1960s, will understand what a frightening prospect this is.

Leadership by gerontocracy contributes to the difficulty. Members seem unwilling to accept the reality that recent age-impaired prophets such as David O. McKay, Spencer W. Kimball, and Ezra Taft Benson have lost any prophetic or cognitive powers due to physical and mental incapacity. This has never been more apparent than when grandson Steve Benson, after visiting his 94-year-old grandfather, declared him to be mentally dysfunctional and unable even to recognize him. His public announcement of this fact was met by the orthodox with incredulity and even death threats.

Those highest-ranking men who direct the church in the prophet/president's absence are also aged. As a result, the leadership, which tightly controls the academic environment at BYU, remains entrenched in old thinking.

LDS leaders may be old, but their seniority has not prevented them from imposing officious pronouncements. They have gone far beyond the traditional religious realms of "morals and values" (to use a Catholic phrase describing the limitations of papal infallibility) to speak authoritatively on almost any subject, including the nature of material reality, traditionally the domain of science. In so venturing, they have spoken many errors (such as pronouncements that men dressed like Quakers lived on the moon, that earthlings would never reach the moon, that the earth is very young, and that the human species has not evolved), diminishing their credibility and the infallibility they assume.

Joseph Smith moderated this idea somewhat in warning that "A prophet is only a prophet when speaking as such," but this caveat is not spoken today. No leader seems willing to qualify Benson's statement, nor can members conceive of their prophet ever speaking outside of his role as prophet.

Similarly, Mormons are limited by their belief in scriptural literalism. Although suspicious of the scriptural integrity of the Bible, Mormons hold the Book of Mormon to be "the most perfect book" ever written and maintain a similar view of the inerrancy of its other scriptures, the Doctrine and Covenants and Pearl of Great Price. However, modern multi-disciplinary scholarship has shown the Book of Mormon to be a nineteenth-century product rather than an ancient document as claimed by Joseph Smith. And the original papyrus manuscripts from which the Pearl of Great Price was "translated" have been shown to contain common writings from the Egyptian Book of the Dead rather than actual writings of Abraham and Moses as claimed by Joseph Smith.

Amid these literalistic box canyons the church finds itself in, it defends its position at the expense of its members, such as the accomplished BYU professor of Asian and Near Eastern languages, David P. Wright. Wright, who was described in his termination notice as an "exceptional young scholar and teacher," was refused tenure in 1988 for his views on the nineteenth-century origins of the Book of Mormon and for his historical-critical view of the Bible which caused him to be skeptical of the accuracy of some of the events described. Widely published and unusually competent in his field, Wright was not fired because of scholarly inadequacies. In fact, he was not even fired for what he taught, for it was admitted that he never taught these unorthodox views to his students. He was fired solely on the basis of his personal and privately-held beliefs.

Another intellectually limiting Mormon belief is the myth of absolute and unchanging doctrine or, as defined in a recent church pronouncement justifying the punishment of heterodox thinkers, "doctrinal purity." Another reference to the Widtsoe-Smith encounter might be instructive here. Although born just four years apart in the 1870s, Widtsoe came to value the progression of knowledge in all fields, while the younger Smith developed a great suspicion if not contempt for non-revealed knowledge. In Smith's view, the truths of science are ever-changing and generally unreliable, while the truths of Mormonism are absolute and unchanging. He was half right.

Science does change and is happy to do so. But religious truths change as well.

In his article, "The Reconstruction of Mormon Doctrine," BYU professor of American history Thomas G. Alexander put to rest the myth that Mormon theology is constant and unchanging by showing the evolution of basic doctrines of God and humankind. Carefully documenting several remarkable changes from 1830 through 1925, Alexander showed that Mormons have understood and worshipped different gods at different times. The godhead Mormons think of now is entirely different in character than the divinity worshipped by early Mormons. Moreover, Mormonism's unchangeable doctrines are changing as we speak. The infusion of ideas from protestant neo-orthodox theology is a recent example.

Not only do church doctrines change, but they sometimes change in ways that negatively affect academic freedom. For example, some LDS leaders seem to be altering the church's traditional views of freedom and choice in adverse ways, as evidenced by Apostle Boyd Packer's recent change of time-honored concept of "free agency" to the more obedience-oriented "moral agency."

Perhaps the single most intellectually confining idea in Mormonism is its belief that it is the only "true church." I believe that any exclusive claim to truth is antithetical to the freedom of thought needed in life generally and in the academy in particular. An often quoted Mormon scripture tells us that the LDS church is "the only true and living church upon the face of the whole earth." We might begin by questioning how a church, which is an organization, can be "true." Perhaps some teachings comprise true propositions, but how can an ever-changing organizational structure be true? Anyone believing in exclusive truth possesses an intellectual arrogance which will prove hostile to those committed to the life of the mind and the on-going search for knowledge, foundation stones of the twentieth-century university.

I believe that Mormons are also overburdened by their conditional view of truth. More than ever before, Mormon leaders are intolerant of unfriendly truths. This has been emphasized by Apostle Russell Nelson, who counseled that truth should not be spoken if it could injure or destroy. Such advice reminds us of the old saying, "If you can't say something nice, don't say anything at all." But what if it is necessary to use truth to expose the injury, unrighteousness, and injustice Nelson is concerned about? Using truth to expose abuse is what Lavina Fielding Anderson did. It resulted in her excommunication.

Elder Dallin Oaks has similarly warned against those "alternate voices" who speak on religious subjects "without calling or authority," reinforcing the idea that the veracity and usefulness of a statement is based not on its inherent truthfulness, but on who pronounced it. Oaks defends the church policy of isolating leaders from speaking or debating in open, public settings. He believes leaders should stay within the safe format of the semi-annual general conference. They should stay away from forums in which their ideas might be questioned or even challenged. He promotes protecting leaders against any accountability for their ideas. In his words, "Members of the church are free to participate or listen to alternate voices they choose (this was obviously several years ago), but church leaders should avoid official involvement, directly or indirectly." His justification is that leaders might be misunderstood. But the context of the address suggests that the real reason is fear that leaders will not be able to control the situation and avoid embarrassment. He dismisses debate as contentious, claiming that truth is better received by the humble "from the Holy Ghost through personal study and quiet contemplation."

Debating societies in every town were important features of earlier Mormonism. These have been completely disposed of. Earlier Mormons were confident in both the strength of their beliefs and the process of open discussion which leads to their discovery and refinement. This confidence has been replaced by the total elimination of dialogue between high-ranking leaders and questioning members. Even study groups, which for generations have enriched the intellectual and spiritual growth of members, have been discouraged or forbidden.

This lack of trust in allowing members to search for truth without supervision extends to the condemnation of independent Mormon forums like the Sunstone Symposia, the Mormon Women's Forum, and other such events. There is a fear that without being spoon-fed "truth" in a controlled setting members might become convinced of new truths which are incompatible with those promoted by the church.

The church is not without cause in harboring these fears. Since its founding, it has lost members who have learned uncomfortable truths about leaders, practices, doctrine and history. Some have been lost to the influences of secularism, rationalism, positivism, socialism, and other worldly competitors of Mormonism. A humanist would say that any person has the right and duty to explore all of these options and select the best from among them. Mormon leaders would argue that their duty is to hide these confusing truths from the members who are childlike and weak and will be eaten by ravening wolves if not protected. Joseph Smith's statement that "We teach the people correct principles and they govern themselves" is a favorite Mormon precept endorsing free will. But if it was ever believed in the past, there is little evidence that it is believed today. A less lofty but more accurate contemporary version is: "We teach them what to believe and punish them if they question it."

In the 1980s, Apostle Oaks presented to the BYU student body a paper entitled, "Reading Church History," in which he warned that it is "improper to criticize leaders, even if the criticism is true." A consistent theme of all recent authoritative LDS treatments of truth is the principle that church-supporting, faith-promoting truths bearing happy faces are welcome; but challenging facts, no matter how important or crucial, are not welcome, and their bearers are in peril of losing their church membership and with it their eternal exaltation.

A favorite Mormon saying is, "When the prophet has spoken, the thinking is done." Leaders control and govern from the top-down and make available no procedure for calling them into accountability for their actions or statements. When abuses of freedom occur, there are no channels for communication, no fair process for appeals. The system is a closed, totalitarian one. Like other authoritarian regimes, Mormonism seems to value coercion more than voluntary action, unity more than diversity, conformity more than individuality, silence rather than expression, obedience more than self-initiative, sacrifice more than responsible service, humility rather than courage, dogmatism rather than open questions, deference more than free inquiry, acceptance more than challenge, positive image more than truth, simplicity more than complexity, submissiveness more than creativity, fiat rather than reasoning, power more than love, and exclusivity more than inclusivity.

The fact that the church is selective about which truths it accepts has ramifications for the educational experience. In a classroom setting, this translates into self-censorship about the kinds of questions asked. I attended five full years at BYU in the late-1960s and early 1970s without being exposed to significant local, national, and global issues and dilemmas, not because I didn't take the right classes—I took a few classes in almost every subject and didn't choose a major until the end of my junior year —but because the issues and dilemmas were not raised. They were not discussed. I studied philosophy at both BYU and the University of Utah and found their respective approaches to the same subject to be quite different.

Mormonism and its educational programs (which are extensive) suffer from limited access to inquiry and knowledge because of censorship and intentional manipulation of its own history. A practice long-carried on by Mormons and other religions, censorship was frequently used by church founder Joseph Smith in an attempt to eliminate opposing ideas. He established an unsettling precedent by ordering the destruction of the *Nauvoo Expositor*, a publishing house which in its only issue exposed the prophet's polygamy. Later, histories of key church figures, such as Joseph and Lucy Smith, were pervasively altered so as to hide unpleasant anomalies. Other important documents, such as William Clayton's Nauvoo, Illinois, journals, records of the Mountain Meadows Massacre, and George Q. Cannon's and Francis M. Lyman's personal journals, were hidden away in the First Presidency's vaults, never to see the light of day. Only occasionally do such records as the personal writings of Joseph Smith and the long-hidden accounts of Nauvoo polygamy fortuitously find their way into print.

In the university setting, limiting the kinds of books placed in the BYU bookstore, library, and classes, together with controlling accepted speakers, entertainers, and movies on campus, constrict students' exposure to the wide world of ideas. Perhaps some lines should be drawn, but the net effect of systematic institutional censorship is that students cannot choose from among disparate ideas available.

They are instead too often directed into pre-determined channels of safe thought.

A practical ramification of this enforced narrowness became evident in a recent *Fortune* article which described Utah as one of the most favorable states in the country in which to establish a new business. The reasons give us pause. Utah employees, they said, are generally hard working and honest, unquestioning, not very creative, and willing to work for low pay.

Diversity is a virtue at most universities. At BYU, it is anathema. The disciplining of three professors in 1911 for their belief in organic evolution was but one precursor of the recent dismissal of heterodox faculty members, David Knowlton and Cecilia Konchar Farr. One effect of intolerance is the loss of diverse and outspoken faculty. Another is the suppression of research because it is not valued. A. C. Lambert, Parley A. Christensen, and Wilford Poulsen are among the faculty who kept their life's works secret rather than publish them and risk chastisement and possible loss of employment.

The advancement of knowledge depends in large part on the intellectual process of questioning old assumptions and methods. Challenging existing authorities is part of this process. When a religious leader demands obedience to a particular edict, whether political, behavioral, or doctrinal, it creates a dilemma for students who are forced to chose between competing and contradictory sources of information. Since religious authority carries the weight of divine approval, the stakes are high for those who believe their eternal status hangs in the balance. Such religious intimidation is sufficient to dissuade many from pursuing truth in areas of study in which the claims of religion may be tested. Unfortunately, most disciplines have ramifications for religious belief. Thus the call to unquestioning obedience stifles most serious intellectual inquiry in a religious context.

The conservative religious agenda tends to limit attempts at objectivity. Objectivity is one of those highly-touted but rarely-achieved goals, yet it can be sought to greater or lesser degree, especially in some fields that lend themselves to quantitative analysis. Efforts to use resources of BYU to prove the validity of LDS practices or beliefs have, for the most part, backfired and resulted in a loss of credibility.

One example comes to mind—a long and expensive attempt by archaeologists in south and central America to prove the ancient veracity of the Book of Mormon. This effort has never succeeded. After decades of research and hundreds of excavations, BYU professor of anthropology Ray T. Matheny concluded in a 1984 paper entitled "Book of Mormon Archeology" that there is no archaeological basis to support the Book of Mormon as ancient Mesoamerican. His scores of convincing examples are too lengthy to mention here. The fact that he was warned not to speak again in public on this issue is the salient point.

BYU is dominated both by religious thinking and conservative ideology, whether religious, political, economic, or social. The church and university readily respond to letters of complaint from conservative parents, students, faculty, and alumni; but they seem to ignore suggestions from the liberal community. For example, faculty members with feminist leanings have been accused and punished for "politicizing courses," the real reason for Cecilia Konchar Farr's firing. Yet long-standing professors have been indoctrinating and politicizing students for decades with all sorts of orthodox social, religious, and political beliefs.

As a BYU student I experienced this personally and learned that it was permissible to teach virtually any sort of nonsense, provided it was conservative, not liberal, nonsense. Academic freedom at BYU is thus one-sided, and the lack of checks and balances creates an environment of intellectual favoritism and inequality in which the dominant position goes unchallenged and brutalizes others: the one has too much power and the others not enough. While some faculty are exceptions and are relatively non-self-censoring, there are still many who will not openly discuss ideas or propositions.

One role of the twentieth-century university is to advance fields of knowledge through research and publishing. The BYU faculty has a poor record in this regard, averaging far fewer publications per person than the national norm. Part of this reflects an ambivalent attitude toward research. Faculty who will not risk expressing themselves, or have no time to research and write, tend to stagnate rather than advance in their disciplines, robbing students of up-to-date information and thinking.

Another role of modern universities has been to be seedbeds of revolutionary doctrines and social progress. As Karl Marx wrote, "The philosophers have only interpreted the world in various ways. Nevertheless, the point is to change it." This axiom has been taken to heart in many university settings. Revolutions of all sorts are important to the advancement of civilization. Leaders are often trained in universities where they obtain ideological foundations, inspired by stories of social change, sensitivity to the human condition, and possibilities for the good society, as taught in social classics such as Plato's *Republic,* the *Federalist Papers* of Jefferson, Madison, et al., and Marx's *Das Kapital.*

It could be argued that in its own quiet way, Mormonism is a radical vehicle of social change, even if it seems to many to be a self-absorbed and self-interested vehicle. Present-day Mormonism seems just as determined to maintain the status quo as early day Mormonism was determined to change society through religious revolution. Those times are long past, and I see little evidence that BYU is producing latter-day revolutionaries interested in addressing the world's ills. Where is the activism and idealism for which great universities are known? Past student efforts, such the distribution of anti-war pamphlets in the 1960s and 1970s, have been squelched, in part through the careful surveillance of all student and faculty activities.

Secret monitoring with intent to harm severely compromises academics at BYU and throughout the church. This practice was made infamous during the long administration of BYU president Ernest L. Wilkinson. In our own times, similar procedures exist. How did trustees obtain information on scholars that led to their eventual censure? It is now apparent that conservative members of the religion faculty, the Foundation for Ancient Research and Mormon Studies, the Church Education System, and the Committee for Strengthening Church Members secretly monitor colleagues and church members at large, collecting verbal and written information on what they consider to be questionable or unorthodox activity. Tapes of speeches and copies of offending articles and manuscripts are brought to the attention of high-ranking leaders and are forwarded to local leaders or university administrators responsible for exacting punishment. In some documented instances, spies have been sent into BYU classrooms. While every university is beset with political intrigue, the church system of secret spying, reporting, recriminating, and then denying (while at the same time justifying) the practice works against academic and intellectual freedom at all levels.

Conflict resolution is not a well-developed discipline at BYU. Controversy is not welcomed, nor are students and professors who engage in it. The overriding need for conformity has led to the creation of review procedures, some of them informal, which inhibit academic freedom.

Decisions about troublesome faculty, for example, too greatly involve the board of trustees and members of upper level administration and too little rely on departmental recommendations. This policy of high level interference runs against the recommendations of the American Association of University Professors. Interference by those not directly knowledgeable about the faculty subverts the principle that academic departments are best qualified to assess the competency and contribution of their members.

The recent handling of the termination of five BYU faculty members illustrates the compromising of academic integrity in favor of orthodoxical purity. More than a year before their dismissal, the names of Cecilia Konchar Farr and David Knowlton appeared in correspondence to university administrators from a member of the board of trustees directing the school to discipline these professors. BYU provost Bruce Hafen confirmed this process during an interview with a BYU newspaper reporter, only to reverse himself later by demanding that the reporter not run the story. Although the university has made much of the fairness and independence of the faculty evaluation procedure with defensive statements in local newspapers, there seems to have been considerable premeditation in these terminations, with one or more trustees interfering from behind the scenes.

Even if members of the Faculty Council on Rank and Status received no specific "marching orders" themselves, their ability to act independently was compromised by the knowledge that their own status would be jeopardized by any action, whether known or imagined, not supportive of the trustees. As a church leader once reminded me, prudent members know that suggestions from Mormon leaders are to be considered as commandments.

BYU president Rex Lee commented publicly that he agreed with the firings even though he knew he would later be asked to provide final judgment in the appeal process. Such prejudice makes a mockery of BYU's scholarship evaluations. That the appeals would be denied was a near-certainty. At its core, the present review process is simply too incestuous and politicized. In a fiercely authoritarian system wherein obedience is the real first principle of church rule, everyone in the system must be an organization man or woman; that is, a yes-man or -woman. To behave otherwise is to be vulnerable to punitive action. Outside, independent review of scholarship would strengthen the credibility of the process, as would a mechanism to neutralize the biases of review committee members who had a record of opposition to individual candidates. But as neither of these provisions for fair and independent review exists at BYU, the current problematic method of censoring scholars remains intact.

In summary, solutions to these problems are difficult. I should acknowledge here that despite its weaknesses, BYU is occasionally capable of uncharacteristic excellence. Moreover, extensive recent literature by the likes of Allan Bloom and others have exposed failures of twentieth-century higher education in general. Still, BYU is in need of significant improvement, starting from the top down. A May 1993 speech by apostle and BYU trustee Boyd Packer named "so-called scholars and intellectuals" as among leading enemies of the church. This kind of rhetoric sends a message to all LDS students weighing the value of pursuing a life of the mind. Packer was the force behind the recent purge of intellectuals. It cannot be overstated that BYU's character is shaped by its trustees.

In a meeting of administrators discussing the image and accreditation concerns due to the terminations of controversial faculty members, one leader commented, "Some things are more important than accreditation." Perhaps so, but BYU's current hybrid, schizophrenic character may be troublesome to maintain over time.

If the church is willing to give up its iron-handed rule, BYU may flourish, as has the University of Notre Dame under the governance of a lay board of trustees composed of a diverse group of citizens, alumni, and educators. As Jackson Newell has observed, "The buffer provided by a lay board would defuse many of the present tensions with intellectuals by separating the parties who hold divergent views on issues like leader infallibility and the sources for knowledge and truth."

A radical measure on the opposite end of the spectrum would be to change the school's role and name to Brigham Young Seminary and make the full transition to a parochial school, giving up the pretense of being a full-fledged university founded on the principle of open inquiry. This would be a bitter pill, and I am one of many who would not like to see this happen.

A middle ground would be to establish a more diverse board and replace the religion department with an off-campus religious program such as exists at non-Mormon colleges worldwide. By making religious instruction a separate, optional activity, and perhaps by instituting an academic religious studies program, the needs of both church and school might be better satisfied.

6.
A Humanist View of Religious Universities

Vern L. Bullough

Both Mormonism and Secular Humanism espouse the value of intelligent thinking, but I am not so sure we define things in the same way. For example, Mormonism has an ambiguous statement, often quoted, that the "Glory of God is Intelligence." I have never been certain what that meant, and particularly whether the term applies only to God or whether it should also apply to humans—that is, that the greatest thing that humans have is intelligence. Humanists would argue the latter, that it is the ability of humans to conceive abstract ideas and to solve problems which separates humans from the higher animals.

Humanists base their belief system on a rational process of arriving at objective truth, namely the scientific method of testing and verifying the empirical world. We do not hold that science gives us final answers, only a method of arriving at a human response to some of life's basic questions. In fact, we emphasize that we do not have an unequivocal perception of ultimate reality; we are not so much afraid of making erroneous assumptions as of perpetuating them. We believe all conjectures should be subjected to the severest imaginable empirical tests, in the hope they will reveal their fallacies. Refutation, however, should be well considered. We hold that a conjecture deserves to be retained at least until contradicted by a successfully tested new hypothesis. Perhaps this is ultimately the key to the concept of academic freedom. Only by continually questioning and challenging perceived truths can we verify or modify them.

Mormons, on the other hand, hold that revealed truth is the highest form of truth, and since God's knowledge, the source of revelation, is greater than human perception, revealed truth supersedes anything arrived at by more primitive rational tests. At base, this concept is inimical to academic freedom. Why question or challenge ideas when the truth is known?

Mormons, however, have an out. Revelation for them is an ongoing process which to me implies that ideas and concepts change. Such change can be explained as a better or more complete or fuller understanding of God's will, but, however it is explained, it seems to imply that truth, or at least what is accepted as truth, is relative, if only because humans remain unable to comprehend all that God knows. Mormonism then comes at the point where, in secular terms, ideas and concepts change, but in religious terms, God's will on new problems is not yet known. The latter is justification for academic freedom, since it can be argued that by questioning and challenging traditional knowledge, we are preparing ourselves to receive a more comprehensive revelation of God's truth. But at this point in time Mormon church authorities often seem too fearful of change to tolerate such discussion.

This is not a problem unique to Mormonism. This is what happened to Marxism under Stalin where truth was what the central committee said it was. The Soviet academic either had to accept what Stalin said or suffer ostracism and punishment.

This to me only emphasizes the importance of academic freedom for both religious and non-religious alike. The ability to challenge traditional concepts, even if the challenge threatens what has passed for revealed truth, has been the key to human progress. Let me put it another way, from the perspective of a knowledgeable outsider. Mormons, like every other organized group, privately hold a variety of opinions among themselves on most issues of the day. Some are liberal, some are conservative, others are radical, and still others are reactionary, although most remain Mormons in good standing. When I was growing up in Salt Lake City, I was most fascinated by talks given by Waldemar Reed, a philosophy professor who was a member of the LDS church. In discussions with him, individuals such as myself wondered how he could remain a member of the LDS church when he held many of the views he did. He argued that he had never yet met a group of people with whom he could agree on everything, that he did not always agree with the LDS church, but overall he felt there was more good than bad. He also held it was his duty to point out failings and contradictions because while at heart Mormonism might be based on revealed truth, most of the time it acted just as any other institution, trying to adjust to the problems of the contemporary world. However, he did not teach at Brigham Young University.

I am sure he represented the view of many so called liberal Mormons. At that time, back in the early 1940s, I was concerned with racial problems and wondered how he could remain a Mormon when on such earth-shaking issues as race, the Mormon church was clearly wrong, reflecting the biases of the nineteenth century and their own problems in Missouri. He agreed the Mormons were wrong and some day would change. He said he could argue his own view more forcefully from within the LDS community than outside it. But his association with what I regarded as a major evil was a view that I could not accept. Ultimately, however, the Waldemar Reeds prevailed and the Mormon church did change.

Did God change his mind on this or on other issues that Mormons once held dear? I am sure that not all changes depend on revelation, but instead are simply necessitated by a growing and expanding organization. When I was growing up in Utah, many people refused to go to movies on Sunday since such a practice had been denounced by church authorities as were many other forms of recreation which took place on Sunday. Now such practices arouse little comment.

As a high school student in Utah I became increasingly aware of the contradictions between church pronouncements and what people did, and as I entered the University of Utah I was not surprised to find out that ideas expressed by professors were often in conflict with those expressed in official church pronouncements. Though some professors were insistent about their rights to express their own views, regarding it as a necessary aspect of academic freedom, most were far more cautious and not interested in making waves. If they could prevent a conflict and keep their integrity, they tried to do so. I was fascinated by the way in which many, both Mormons and non-Mormons, dealt with the overwhelming presence of the church in Utah.

One of the best examples occurred when I attempted to take a course in evolutionary biology. Though the church itself is based on a concept of evolution—humans evolving to become gods—there was official concern that organic evolution denied the special creation of humans. Although the catalogue listed a course entitled "Evolution," and such a class had briefly existed, it was no longer offered on a regular basis. It was, however, available through self-study. Thus the university kept its independence, the students who wanted to learn more about evolution could do so, but open detailed classroom discussion was avoided by having the self-study option. I am certain that if a professor had wanted to make an issue of this timid approach, the course would again have been regularly taught, as it later was. No faculty members at the university wanted to force such a confrontation at that time.

Traditionally there has been a belief among religious conservatives that religious ideas do not change. In the minds of Christian fundamentalists, the words of Jesus mean the same now as they did nearly two millennia ago. Mormons for their part admit to change, which gives them an advantage over Biblical literalists; because the issues of modern America are not those of ancient Palestine. They believe in the Bible insofar as it is translated correctly, a position which leaves plenty of room for maneuver on issues of biblical meaning and sources. Joseph Smith himself attempted to rewrite the Bible, correcting its errors in what is sometimes called the Inspired Version. The Reorganized Church of Jesus Christ of Latter Day Saints, embraced by Joseph Smith's family who refused to follow Brigham Young west, retained the copyright to this biblical revision. Other Mormon scriptures have been revised, such as the Book of Mormon, Doctrine and Covenants, and Pearl of Great Price. This gives Mormons an advantage over biblical literalists, because the issues of modern America are not those of ancient Palestine. Usually, however, it is not differences in material culture on which religions are conservative, but the world of ideas. Still, religions gradually change, some at a faster pace than others.

Change, however, poses problems since if religions conform too much to the secular world, their members see little need to belong, able to satisfy the needs previously filled by churches with other groups. This appears most evident in the decline in mainstream Protestantism which probably has been the most accommodating to modern issues. It also appears among humanists, most of whom do not belong to organized humanist groups. No wonder many denominations have fought against change; and, in the case of fundamentalists, gone to great lengths to insist on biblical literalness. Some of these groups who insist on a narrow, rigid definition of orthodoxy seem to be growing, although they are selective of the scriptures they use and lack any historical sense of early Christianity. Growth, however, is usually short-lived for those who are so narrowly rigid, and even the narrowest find it necessary to bend with the times.

For example, the old order Amish refuse to use buttons on their clothes because they are not mentioned in the Bible, but then neither are paper, ink, buggies, combines, tractors, and other things. Somehow buttons became the symbol while buggies did not. The Amish are not alone in their selection of which biblical statements are fundamental to their conduct.

Insistence on biblical literalness has led Southern Baptists to purge their seminaries of so-called liberals and some Lutheran synods have followed a similar path. Similar attempts to reject modern secularism have occurred in Catholicism under Pope John Paul II. Though they may rely on purges of faculty and bishops to keep clergy orthodox, or at least quiescent, they do not keep modern secularist ideas from creeping in among the laity. Mormons, however, have a particular problem which differs from Catholics, Baptists, or Lutherans in that there is no separation between clergy and lay because in Mormonism all males age twelve and up hold priesthood. This difference has particular meaning for BYU.

Traditionally, universities developed as training grounds for clergy. In the Middle Ages every student in the university was by definition a cleric. Secular universities were for the most part a development of the nineteenth century, although even before that time the nature of education had begun to change. In the United States, though private colleges had been organized by religious denominations to educate clergy (Cornell was a major exception), non-clerical students were soon admitted. Harvard was established to train clergy, and when it came to be regarded as too liberal, a group of dissenters founded Yale.

There was really no academic freedom in these early institutions, although college professors since the time of St. Thomas Aquinas had been challenging traditional ideas. Academic freedom is a twentieth-century development. For a brief period the writings of Aquinas were labeled as heretical. Martin Luther was a theological professor, and when he broke with Catholicism, so did his university. As churches found it more difficult to control professors, particularly as colleges became something more than a training ground for clergy, they turned to special seminaries in which orthodoxy was emphasized and required. This was a major factor in the development of academic freedom, if only because the battleground to maintain orthodoxy shifted from the university to the seminary. Some seminaries even seceded from universities which had grown too secular.

Even seminaries, however, did not prove immune to the contagion of new ideas. Faculty felt it was important to educate students in the thinking of the non-religious world. To do so they turned to what came to be called Higher Criticism. This liberal religious scholarship troubled many denominations, who either tried to enforce orthodoxy in their seminaries or refused to ordain graduates who did not accept what they regarded as orthodox beliefs. Religious scholarship, however, was not usually preached in sermons as professionals sought to avoid antagonism with their congregations or church hierarchies. Still, standards of belief changed.

The more rigidly orthodox have renewed their attempts to control what is taught in their seminaries, trying to close their doors to modernism. The result has been a series of heresy trials, particularly in Missouri Synod Lutheran and Southern Baptist seminaries. Most of these are not accredited by regular college standards and rely on denominational acceptance. Some churches have established colleges where the whole faculty must adhere to narrow guidelines of orthodoxy, but they do so only by refusing tax money, something that only the zealous are willing to do. Therefore, instead of growing, the number of religiously controlled colleges has declined. Even Catholic Colleges reorganized themselves with lay boards of trustees and became officially non-sectarian in order to get public funds even though they continued to bear such names as Loyola or St. Mary's.

This secularization of American colleges has meant that questions of orthodoxy have focused increasingly on religious professionals, rather than on members of the congregation. As a result, the concept of academic freedom has spread beyond secular institutions and high status private schools to vast areas of academia recently freed from dogmatic control. Seminaries, however, pose special problems since large numbers are still controlled by religious bodies.

All of this is by way of background to the growing problems faced by Brigham Young University. The fact that Mormonism lacks a professional clergy only accentuates the problem. Prophets and apostles are called from the laity. These general authorities attribute gospel interpretation to inspiration from God; few are experts in biblical studies or theology. Because the Mormon church emphasizes longevity as the prerequisite for becoming a new prophet, it also means that leaders are not up to date on current issues of scholarship or scientific findings. All the leaders of the Mormon church from Joseph Smith to the current prophet, Ezra Taft Benson, were born in the nineteenth century, and though many attended colleges or universities, such institutions were far more parochial than they now are. As administrators, few church leaders have time to dig into major questions of theology. Instead, what they do is interpret events through their own prisms which according to Mormonism are guided by inspiration and occasionally revelation, but to outsiders they seem to reflect the attitudes of the generations when the Mormon leaders were coming of age. Neither old age nor senility has been addressed as a problem.

Moreover, since all devout adult male members hold priesthood, any deviant member who becomes prominent can pose a threat similar to that of a deviant priest or minister in other churches. In fact, women, who only hold the priesthood through their husbands, pose the greatest threat because they challenge the very basis of control.

Often in the past the Mormon church was slow to excommunicate ordinary members who did not threaten the church directly. From my time in Utah I knew individuals who begged the church to excommunicate them, who joined other churches to emphasize their break with Mormonism, and even slammed the door in the faces of home teachers and in one case met them with a shotgun;

but most of these people were kept on church rolls regardless of their personal preference. Increasingly, however, this is not the case; in recent decades church leaders have not only been willing to let individuals remove themselves from membership but have become more aggressive in threatening excommunication. They have been particularly concerned about orthodoxy in their institutions, of which BYU is the most influential. BYU and other Mormon colleges are unique in that they are both seminaries and universities. In order to preserve its independence, BYU has refused to accept federal funds and any policy requirements that go with them. Faculty are almost always Mormons in good standing who pay tithing and not only attend religious services regularly but are active participants in them.

Yet at the same time BYU aspires to become a leader in higher education, and because many Mormons want to live in Utah, it has managed to attract some particularly distinguished scholars. BYU is also a source of conflict, because religious orthodoxy and intellectual freedom have not mixed well in recent times.

One enormous problem is that it is not always clear to Mormons what orthodoxy is, and defining orthodoxy becomes a matter of politics. People get into influential positions and define orthodoxy as what they say it is. Religions have their Stalins, and when a dogmatist achieves a powerful position, academic freedom is in peril. Though none of those in the LDS church hierarchy has yet to entertain Stalinist fantasies, they speak as "general authorities" on subjects they know little about, claiming a special relationship with God as authority. Sometimes the Council of the Twelve Apostles quietly leashes some of its colleagues, but this is rare. Who but a general authority can say when a colleague has started to read his own prejudices into doctrine? This is one of the purposes that academic freedom is supposed to serve, following the principles in John Stuart Mill's classic essay "On Liberty" of putting accepted truth to the challenges of criticism.

Excommunication, the ultimate threat to the believer, which was, until recently, used primarily against reactionary members, is now being used to control BYU faculty. Mormon church officials, like many of their Muslim counterparts, have awakened to the dangers of heresy and in the latest wave of excommunications have exiled both liberal critics and arch conservatives. The result has been a growth of what can only be called a siege mentality among the Mormon hierarchy. Use of excommunication to control dissent is like an alcoholic taking the first drink. Once an institution starts a purge when can it stop? Dissent is regarded as dangerous, and open disagreement treacherous. Academic freedom itself becomes the threat, criticism the enemy. I suspect that few people have the courage to resist, and while dissenters might be urged on, few of BYU faculty will join them. From my perspective, academic freedom and BYU now seem like an oxymoron.

As a humanist, I can only sympathize with my besieged colleagues. I do not, however, assert that humanists are free from problems. In part, we have avoided it because we do not control any institution of higher education and our national bodies are competitive with each other. Sometimes I almost wish we could excommunicate some who call themselves humanists. This only emphasizes why academic freedom is so important, to protect us from ourselves.

In some parts of the world, where humanism is institutionalized, the same kind of issues present themselves. In the Netherlands, for example, where the government gives money to religious groups for social services and education, humanists have established college-level schools to train professionals as social workers, counsellors, etc. Since religiously-oriented professionals are given course work in religion, humanists similarly have to get training in humanism. Committed to academic freedom, the founders of the University of Humanism hired experts in various fields of philosophy to teach classes, and it turns out that most are fashionably into deconstructionism, the denial of the value of the scientific method, and an emphasis on aesthetics. Some even seem to believe in God. In sum, perhaps we secular humanists avoid the problems of academic freedom faced by Mormon academics at BYU by not having our own institutions in the United States.

My heart goes out to my BYU friends and I know from firsthand experience some of their feelings and emotions, since I myself was once an academic freedom "case" and for a time was threatened with loss of employment. Though I won my case, I resigned anyway, and went on to better things. At the time it was going on, it was hell.

Whether BYU will have academic freedom in the long run is something only the faculty can determine. The Mormon church also has to decide whether it wants a first-class academic institution or a third-rate college more concerned with orthodoxy than intellectual frontiers. Outsiders can only criticize and empathize. The decision ultimately is a Mormon one. As of this writing, academic freedom and BYU seem to form an oxymoron.

7.

Academic Freedom
Forever; However . . .

Frederick S. Buchanan

The present tensions at Brigham Young University are due to a perceived need to hold faculty accountable to a dual standard. In my experience as a member of a retention, promotion, and tenure committee at the University of Utah, making decisions on the future of one's colleagues is difficult enough in an institution which is committed to pursuit of "objective truth." To add to this, the extent to which scholarship or behavior conforms to "divine truth" compounds an already daunting task. BYU is attempting to be both a seminary devoted to faith and a university devoted to, in Jefferson's words, the pursuit of "truth wherever it may lead." The central question of this dialogue is: Can Brigham Young University be a religious school and still promote and preserve academic freedom?

I began thinking about this last summer while attending a six-week National Endowment for the Humanities institute on Jefferson at "Mr. Jefferson's University" in Charlottesville, Virginia, and at his alma mater, the College of William and Mary in Williamsburg. My readings about Jefferson confirmed a suspicion about where the discussion might lead: the tension between Jeffersonian ideals and Jefferson's practices.

If anyone epitomizes the ideal of academic freedom it is surely the "Sage of Monticello." After all, this is the humanist who "swore eternal hostility against every form of tyranny over the minds of men." Consider too Jefferson's paean to freedom which he said characterized the University of Virginia. The university, he wrote at its founding, "will be based on the illimitable freedom of the human mind. For here we are not afraid to follow truth wherever it may lead, nor to tolerate any error so long as reason is left free to combat it."[1] However, when one looks further, the "darker side" of Jefferson's perspective comes into view. For instance, when asked how David Hume's Tory-oriented *History of England* might be safely used by American students, Jefferson recommended that to prevent students from "sliding into Federalist doctrine" the editor should "give you the text of Hume, purely and verbally, till he comes to some misrepresentation or omission . . . he then alters the text silently, *makes it say what truth and candor say it should be*, and resumes the original text again as soon as it becomes innocent, without having warned you of your rescue from misguidance."[2] Again when the time came for Jefferson to choose the faculty of law, he was not reluctant to favor Republican rather than Federalist perspectives. He did not want the Revolution to be subverted by "wrong" Federalist ideology and felt justified in censoring "wrong" texts and curtailing those who espoused "wrong" principles. He had his own view of political correctness or "political purity" and imposed it on his university in the name of a higher end—namely, the survival of Republican institutions. I suppose he could even have claimed that such indoctrination made his university a freer place to study the "truth" about the new nation.[3]

I cite these instances not to rationalize such actions or provide Jeffersonian legitimacy for the curtailment of academic freedom, but to illustrate the complexity of the issue of ends and means, of ideals and realities. Indeed, I was reminded of my mentor, Lowell L. Bennion, discussing at the Salt Lake City LDS Institute of Religion adjacent to the University of Utah the difference between ideals and reality. He drew a straight line across the board and said, "This is the ideal world. The world we aspire to." Below the straight line he drew

---

1. Cited in Merrill D. Peterson, *Thomas Jefferson and the New Nation* (New York: Oxford University Press, 1970), 987.

2. Cited in David B. Tyack, ed., *Turning Points in American Educational History* (Waltham, MA: Blaisdell Publishing Co., 1967), 87-88. Emphasis added.

3. Peterson, *Thomas Jefferson*, 985-86.

a fluctuating graph. This uncertain line, he said, "is how we really act." Jefferson believed in high ideals of freedom of expression, but his ideals were conditioned by jagged "howevers." And in lesser mortals the same conditions certainly are evident.

The issue of academic freedom at BYU appeared in the *Washington Post* while I was in Virginia and led to considerable discussion with many of the twenty-five academicians from a variety of state and private colleges. Even from those at private religious institutions there was general agreement on the desirability and necessity of academic freedom for faculty *and* students. But once again my colleagues, after expressing general support for academic freedom, would invariably add the ubiquitous "however."

Private, religious institutions are less compelled by tradition and necessity to honor free thought as part of faculty hiring agreements. In large measure such institutions depend on the financial support of a particular ideological community. They actually operate on the basis of "he who pays the piper, calls the tune."

It is within the legal and educational rights of privately supported schools to require that faculty *forego* open criticisms of the policies of the sponsoring institution. And of course similar realities exist at secular institutions.

Most of my colleagues at the Jefferson Institute had difficulty understanding why a person would want to teach at an institution with a special religious mission if they did not concur with the institution's statement of mission. A personal anecdote might illustrate this latter issue. In the 1960s I was invited to consider an appointment at BYU. In the exchange of letters it became evident that BYU president Ernest Wilkinson's role in spying on faculty and the church's stand on denying the priesthood to African-Americans were obstacles. The dean, whose frankness I have come to appreciate, concluded our correspondence by saying: "I think if I were you that I would be reluctant to come to BYU. I think I can see an inescapable conflict between the one paramount obligation of a BYU faculty (that is, not to harm the testimony of the students) and your views. [Your questions] would impel you to some sort of collision."[4]

---

4. Letter to Frederick S. Buchanan, 25 Feb. 1969.

He was right and I think BYU and I were both better off in the long term. The point is, of course, that people who accept a position at any university should fully understand the terms of the contract. At the same time the institution has an obligation to be "up front" about its expectations. Many problems at religious institutions could be prevented if there were clear-cut guidelines and up-front statements of expectations as well as respect for due process and minimal external interference from the Holy See or LDS church headquarters.

Private institutions are not alone in requiring "correct" expression, however: one colleague at the Jefferson Institute had been forced out of his department at a state university because he espoused a conservative ideology. He got an appointment in a religiously-oriented college. The old joke in the John F. Kennedy era: "How do you get to Washington, D.C.? Go to Harvard and turn left" has a serious undertow to it.

As much as I support the ideal of academic freedom, in the perspective of cultural pluralism it appears that something valuable may be lost if universities sponsored by churches are forced to only admit as "truth" that which can be empirically validated and tested by traditional western intellectual standards. The special mission claimed by some religious institutions is even recognized by the accreditation agencies. If historian David Tyack is correct in asserting that there has never been "one best system" of public education in America, surely it is even more evident that there is no "one best system" in higher education.[5] At least as I understand it there is no one infallible scientific method, no one best literary standard, and certainly no one best way to reform education. This is not to say that "anything goes." It does mean, however, that openness to new ideas and methodologies should be a paramount requirement for all institutions of higher education, without these schools being required by external or internal pressure to standardize the search for "truth."

In my conversations at the College of William and Mary I became keenly aware of the diversity of perspectives which exist in Catholic institutions, many of whose boards consist of lay members of the

---

5. David B. Tyack, *The One Best System: A History of American Urban Education* (Cambridge, MA: Harvard University Press, 1974), 11.

Catholic church *and* non-Catholics. Some even have atheists on their faculty as part of their mission statement to follow truth wherever it leads and to allow students to engage in free and open debate. Catholic-oriented colleges do not assume that their prime responsibility is the promotion of official Catholic doctrine or protection of the church from its critics. However, one Utah Catholic educator noted that the increasing secularization of the nominally Catholic colleges is giving many Catholics cause for concern. If Catholic colleges lose their distinctive role and *raison d'etre*, lay people are asking, why bother supporting them?[6]

The irony is that Mormonism supports free inquiry. I grew up hearing numerous Mormon sermons about freedom and the necessity of making choices. One hymn led me, rightly or wrongly, to believe that Mormonism was not incompatible with the freedom to inquire: "Freedom and reason make us men./ Take these away, what are we then?/ Mere animals and just as well/ The beasts may think of heaven or hell."[7]

Nothing so powerfully illustrates Mormon founder Joseph Smith's relative openness to debate and inquiry as an incident at Nauvoo, Illinois, in 1843. A group of over-zealous high priests took

---

6. The celebrated case of Charles Curran at Catholic University of America is a counter-instance of the openness to inquiry that characterizes many Catholic institutions. It is my understanding, however, that this was because CU was in fact an officially designated "Pontifical College" which means that is has been in a sense "accredited" by the Holy See to promote scholarly, but orthodox, interpretations of Catholic doctrine and practices. Faculty in the theology department have, therefore, an obligation *not* to contradict the officially pronounced doctrines or policies of the papacy. Paradoxically, Curran could have done the same critical exegesis on birth control and celibacy in the sociology department. He could not, however, do this as an accredited theologian, because he would then have been teaching with the imprimatur of Rome. Curran was certainly not teaching what Rome wanted him to teach. His efforts to have the courts intervene and reinstate him as a professor of theology failed.

7. "Know This That Every Soul is Free," *Hymns of the Church of Jesus Christ of Latter-day Saints* (Salt Lake City: Church of Jesus Christ of Latter-day Saints, 1985), 240.

one of their number to task for having "wrong" ideas about a verse in the biblical book of Revelation. They were about to put Pelatiah Brown on trial, when Smith stopped the proceedings. Commenting about the incident later he said: "I did not like the old man being called up for erring in doctrine. It looks too much like the Methodists and not like the Latter-day Saints. Methodists have creeds which a man must believe or be asked out of their church. *I want the liberty of thinking and believing as I please. It feels so good not to be trammelled.*"[8] A trammel is, of course, something which everybody in 1842 was familiar with: a hobble or shackle used to make a horse amble instead of run—a means of impeding the horse's freedom and keeping it from straying. Smith wanted the freedom to "lengthen his stride" instead of being restrained to a slow walk. Indeed, Mormon church president Spencer W. Kimball's challenge to "lengthen our stride" in all areas of life is impossible if we're forced to wear a trammel, no matter how comfortable it might be.

There is a strong psychological connection between learning and tension. Dewey held that we learn only when we are solving problems and that puzzlement is a necessary condition of the learning process. My son used to wear a T-shirt to his high school weight-lifting class which read "No Pain—No Gain." It appears to me that there is a close relationship between the notion of intellectual pain or puzzlement and the Mormon notion of free agency and that "there is opposition in all things."[9] How can there be opposition and choice, if, *a priori,* certain things cannot be talked about or written about? In addition to Dewey, learning theories based on the work of Kohlberg and Perry focus on the struggle which must take place in order for humans to develop intellectually, socially, morally, even spiritually.[10] Students

---

8. Joseph Smith., Jr., *History of the Church of Jesus Christ of Latter-day Saints,* Vol. 5 (Salt Lake City: Deseret Book Co., 1949), 340, emphasis added.

9. 2 Ne. 2:11, in Book of Mormon.

10. John Dewey, *How We Think: A Restatement of the Relation of Reflective Thinking to the Educative Process* (Boston: Heath, 1933); Lawrence Kohlberg, *The Psychology of Moral Development* (San Francisco: Harper & Row, 1984); William G. Perry, Jr., *Forms of Intellectual and Ethical Development in the College Years* (New York: Holt, Rinehart & Winston, Inc., 1970).

need to be presented with ideas and arguments slightly beyond their reach so that they are stretched into solving problems and thereby develop capabilities. This is certainly a far cry from B. F. Skinner's operant conditioning and the traditional didactic and catechistical approach to teaching. But then I don't think Mormons have ever put much stock in a no-risk theology which guarantees salvation. Granted that it's messy and uncomfortable, nevertheless risk-taking and choice-making are essential parts of the Mormon view of life which support the ideal of academic freedom.

Over the years a significant amount of sound research has been produced at BYU. I can't dismiss this scholarly output in the sciences, history, sociology, or literature as dishonest, simply because it was done at BYU. I have found much of the research done by my colleagues at the "Y" to be stimulating. This is why I am profoundly saddened that many of them are being measured for a trammel.

To be upbeat for a moment, here are some instances of protection of academic freedom at BYU. When Professor Warner Woodworth in organizational behavior criticized the policies of a local industrial plant, attempts were made by industrial and political interests "to shut him up" for going public with his criticism. The administration resisted the pressures to censure him.[11]

Sociologist Wilford Smith once took issue with capital punishment in a radio address. Later he debated the issue publicly with a member of the religion faculty who said that Smith's position was contrary to church doctrine. A BYU student wrote to the student newspaper urging Smith's dismissal. University president Ernest Wilkinson wrote him saying he appreciated the reasonableness of his presentation and congratulating him for taking a stand "on an important issue on which the last word had not yet been said."[12] Professor Smith believed that "if there is any church that teaches its members to stand on their own feet and to think for themselves it is the Church of Jesus Christ of Latter-day Saints."[13] He once told

---

11. Conversation with Warner Woodworth, 30 July 1992.

12. Wilford E. Smith to Frederick S. Buchanan, 8 Oct. 1993.

13. Letter of Wilford E. Smith in *Dialogue: A Journal of Mormon Thought* 26 (Summer 1993): viii.

Apostle Joseph Fielding Smith that the conservative churchman had driven away more people from the church as a result of his strict teachings than anything he had ever taught at BYU. In a good natured riposte, Apostle Smith responded that he didn't have to get mad about it![14] This feistiness is a healthy antidote to the all-too-common deference and reverence for authority. I'm convinced that some faculty stay at BYU to subvert, in the best educational sense of the word, the rigidity that sets in when people stop thinking critically. In the words of BYU's Parley Christensen, these faithful dissidents prefer to believe that "God himself is limited when [humans] cease to think."[15]

Clearly, some freedom does exist at BYU, but as one BYU faculty member observed to me, "It can be 'bonkersville' down here at times." There is too much "sweetness and light" in the examination of crucial social and religious issues and a definite lack of open clashes of different perspectives. This is partly due to the Mormon need for unity and aversion to controversy. In fact, some view the current trouble as an inevitable cultural clash between provincial rural Utah and a cosmopolitan university. Frequently the rural ambience of the campus is assumed to be the ideal. Situated as BYU is in one of the most conservative counties in the nation, it would be surprising if this tension didn't erupt from time to time.

When I asked a friend who teaches church history at BYU if there were any problems in the department of religious education he said there were no problems whatsoever because the fifty men and one woman who teach there are all of one mind and speak with one voice. When I suggested that at some universities if two people think alike, one of them wasn't necessary, he simply smiled. I suppose he could justify such unanimity among the religion faculty with the scriptural injunction that "If ye are not one, ye are not mine."

A Catholic educator recently observed that BYU was in fact Mormonism's equivalent of a Pontifical College and that like similar

---

14. Wilford Smith related this incident to me in a telephone conversation on 1 Oct. 1993.

15. Parley A. Christensen, *Of a Number of Things* (Salt Lake City: University of Utah Press), 25.

Catholic institutions its main role was to research and explain the orthodox teachings of the church—not to challenge what had already been decided upon by those in authority. Certainly that seems to have been in the mind of church leader J. Reuben Clark, Jr., when he gave the official charge at the inauguration of Howard S. McDonald as president of BYU in 1945. Acknowledging the dual function of BYU in promoting secular and spiritual knowledge, Clark asserted that secular learning is the lesser and spiritual the greater, because spiritual learning "is built upon absolute truth. . . . *These ultimate truths may not be questioned. All secular truths will, must, conform to these ultimate truths.*"[16]

Clark's perspective of lesser and greater truths supports the common notion that *all* of BYU's academic departments are really ancillary to the "unified" religion department. It also promotes the view that the religion faculty are in fact "emissaries of the Brethren." These perspectives make the issue of academic freedom more problematic than in academic departments at Catholic colleges. Ironically in the same issue of the *Improvement Era* which published Clark's charge to McDonald, an article by Marvin O. Ashton, of the Presiding Bishopric of the LDS church, advocated that young people should be taught to think for themselves when giving talks in church instead of parroting what their parents have written for them. He concludes: "Let us not raise parrots—let us, with the inspiration of our Heavenly Father, develop devout thinkers."[17]

It is not in religion alone that absolutes are claimed. I recall one BYU professor of child development in the 1960s saying something like "If a teacher knows what the truth is there is absolutely nothing wrong with indoctrination." The inquiring mind might want to ask a further question: "What is truth?" And what of "creativity, adventure, progress and risk"?[18] Education at a university is not a means to

---

16. J. Reuben Clark, Jr., "Charge to President Howard S. McDonald at his Inauguration as President of the Brigham Young University," *Improvement Era* 49 (Jan. 1946): 60, emphasis added.

17. Marvin O. Ashton, "Poll Parrots or Thinkers," *Improvement Era* 49 (Jan. 1946): 58-59.

18. Sterling M. McMurrin, "Some Distinguishing Characteristics of

promoting a particular point of view, but of asking why such a point of view should be held. Surely it is possible to give good reasons for faith commitments and still remain open to "further light and knowledge," unless, of course, we really do adhere to blind faith, which is not a Mormon tenet. To the contrary, it appears to me that their whole emphasis is on "faith [as] an instrument of growth, not an obligation to stagnation."[19] Indeed, one BYU professor of history, William J. Snow, even suggested at the semi-centennial celebration of the university that "upon many questions of importance it may be that skepticism is the highest of duties and that faith is the unpardonable sin." Uncritical acceptance of political, social and even religious affirmations, Snow averred, "lead to a lethargic and closed mind and block the wheels of progress."[20]

The discussion of academic freedom among the Mormons should include the University of Utah. The first president of the latter, John R. Park, a respected Mormon educator, laid out what can be interpreted as the university's charter in his message to the class of 1879:

> This is your university. . . . The faculty is here to help you to help yourselves. It is a democratic university, which means that every student must share with the faculty the responsibility of conducting it and must cooperate in every way possible for its welfare and success. Each of you will have the right to full and free expression of his thoughts and no opinion or beliefs will be forced upon you.[21]

Lest one assume that this grand vision for the university was consistently upheld, in 1915 a number of faculty were fired for making statements critical of Joseph Smith and the Mormon church.

Mormon Philosophy," *Sunstone* 16 (Mar. 1993): 44.

19. I was unable to find a printed source for this quotation. In my personal notes (c. 1959) I attributed it to Joseph F. Smith, president of the LDS Church from 1901-18. I may have picked the quotation up from T. Edgar Lyon at the Salt Lake Institute of Religion.

20. Snow's comments were made as the representative of the faculty at the Semi-Centennial Dinner on 16 Oct., 1925. See *Utah Genealogical and Historical Magazine* 17 (Jan. 1926):102.

21. Cited in Elizabeth Haglund, ed., *Remembering: The University of Utah* (Salt Lake City: University of Utah Press, 1981), vii, emphasis added.

If I may be permitted a personal incursion here: it was at the U that I first faced the need to think actively about religion. Around 1957 I took a class in political science from Frank Jonas who used a text edited by his colleague G. Homer Durham, entitled *Introductory Readings in Political Science*. Jonas's probing in-class discussions and Durham's provocative questions following each set of readings challenged my patience. As a twenty-four-year-old former LDS missionary, ex-GI, and sophomore, I had never been pushed to this extent before and I resented it. I wanted more facts, not unanswerable questions. In short, I wanted to be catechized. After class one day I confronted Frank Jonas and told him that I was confused by his continual barrage of unanswerable questions. He thereupon introduced me to the essence of the university when he said I shouldn't be so impatient to get immediate answers. When I said I didn't know where we were going in class, he said, "Wait until we get to the end and you'll know where we've been." When I persisted, he glared at me over glasses perched on the end of his nose and growled: "What do you want me to do? Bear my testimony to you?" To Frank Jonas and, ironically, to G. Homer Durham, who later became an LDS general authority, I am indebted for awakening in me the realization that education is more than the dissemination of facts and that there are ethical/religious implications to every field of study.

In 1970 I returned to the university as a faculty member in the department of educational studies. For twenty-three years I have had utmost freedom to pursue what I have construed to be an appropriate program of research in the history of education in Utah. Even when I strayed from a strict focus on educational history and dabbled in Scottish-Mormon studies, every chairperson in our department has given me leeway to follow my line of historical inquiry. Nor could I ask for greater support from the almost totally non-Mormon faculty. At times I have taught classes dealing with religion and education and always included discussion of religion in my classes on American history of education. I have never been cautioned or questioned on the appropriateness of such discussion.

However, the University of Utah has its own set of problems. It is almost impossible for a devout Mormon to find employment in many departments. This unwritten exclusionary policy may reflect a faculty desire to give the U a less regional profile. There may also be a suspicion on the part of non-Mormons that the religious bias of LDS faculty will interfere with research in some areas—a view which recent church disciplinary actions against LDS intellectuals tends to strengthen. But there is also undeniable prejudice. Former director of the Stewart Laboratory School Dr. Roald Campbell told me that in the 1950s highly qualified Mormon applicants were rejected in favor of less qualified non-Mormons. During a discussion in one department of a prospective appointee who had a Mormon background, a faculty member commented that he would never vote to appoint anyone who had "ever breathed the air of Utah." The comment was roundly applauded by other members of the faculty. One friend quipped that he was too good a Mormon for the U and not devout enough for BYU. Similarly students are often wary of how they express themselves in their papers for fear of arousing an instructor's antipathy to Mormon beliefs and getting a low grade. Such students are careful to hide their Mormon values. In so doing they feel that their academic freedom is restricted.

Academia among Mormons, then, is a complex phenomenon. But in spite of all the "howevers" I have used to moderate my position, I believe that Mormonism officially endorses untrammeled scholarship while unfortunately promoting an atmosphere of suspicion and distrust. I think I can understand some of the rationale for such a climate—institutions have a hard time letting go of their children. And yet "letting go," even in the face of risk, is a basic principle of the Mormon world view.

I am reminded of a perceptive Amish teacher who was censured by his church in Ohio for promoting "higher education" (i.e., high school) among the young. An Amish bishop held that this would induce apostasy. The teacher's response was that the church dropout rate among those who *never* went to high school was just as great as among those who went beyond the elementary grades. The same can be said of Mormons. While it is generally held that exposure to higher education decreases the extent of religious activity, among Mormons the more educated are more likely to be active in church. While there is some decrease in "religiosity" among women who go beyond college graduation, in general increased education for Mormon men and woman does *not* increase the degree of secularization they experience. There is greater chance of "backsliding" among mechanics and policemen than among social scientists and educators.[22]

I believe that there is a deeply rooted Mormon belief in free agency. In the spirit of the "creative tension" which Mormon historian Leonard Arrington has said characterizes Brigham Young University, perhaps it is possible for a creative (rather than a dogmatic) resolution of an issue which threatens to parochialize Mormon education. Catholic sociologist Thomas O'Dea said many years ago that Mormonism needs its intellectuals. Today it needs them more than ever if it is to meet the challenges of a worldwide church at the portals of the twenty-first century. John Dewey, who admired much of Mormon social philosophy, trenchantly expressed the need for educational freedom as a means of enhancing the future when he observed that:

> Without light, a people perish. Without freedom, light grows dim and darkness comes to reign . . . Without freedom, old truths become so stale worn that they cease to be truths and become mere dictates of external authority. He who would put the freedom of others in bond, especially the freedom of inquiry and communication, creates conditions which finally imperil his own freedom and that of his offspring.[23]

Hopefully out of a dialogue between Mormons and humanists can emerge a commitment on the part of people of good will to find creative ways of moving beyond "however" toward a more resolute "therefore." Difficult as this may be, surely if Israel and the PLO can resolve the issues which divide them, there is hope for us. The motto of Mormon education should then read: "The Glory of God is Intelligence: It feels so good not be trammelled."

---

22. Stan L. Albrecht and Tim B. Heaton, "Secularization, Higher Education and Religiosity," *Review of Religious Research* 26 (Sept. 1984): 43-58: Tim B. Heaton, "Are Social Scientists Less Religious?" *AMCAP Journal* 13 (1987): 139-43.

23. John Dewey, "Academic Freedom," in *Intelligence in the Modern World: John Dewey's Philosophy*, ed. Joseph Ratner (New York: Modern Library, 1939), 725.

8.
Tenure as a Tool

F. Ross Peterson

My memory takes me back to May 1970, to the University of Texas at Arlington where I taught history. Shortly after the tragic deaths at Kent State and Jackson State colleges, activist students, black and white, wanted a memorial service. After considerable discussion between administrators and students, they agreed on a program and a main speaker. I was asked to be the speaker. My record on civil rights, the Vietnam War, and student issues was public and fairly clear, so both sides agreed on the choice.

The morning before the service, my department chair, E. C. Barksdale, called me into his office. He said, "Do you know what in the hell you are doing?" Barksdale had been fired by a Texas school district in 1937 for organizing teachers. He was crusty, profane, and unforgettable. I responded, "Yes, sir, I do." He slowly pulled out his tobacco pouch, tore off a sheet of cigarette paper from a small pad, silently and sloppily rolled a cigarette, smashed it a little, then lit it. I waited. Then he said, "Be careful."

I responded, "I'm not worried—I've got Academic Freedom." He squinted, "How long you been here?" He knew. "Two years," I answered. His eyes lit up, his clenched fist hit the desk, and he growled, "If those students get carried away and the cops get tough—you ain't got shit!" The memorial service was without incident.

As an undergraduate at Utah State University in Logan, I ran into the issue of tenure as it pertained to Brigham Young University. Numerous faculty had previously been BYU instructors. I learned of firings over organic evolution in the early 1900s. Lowry Nelson, founder of rural sociology as an academic field, left under duress in the 1920s, and others followed. Closer to my academic lifetime was the disruption caused by President Ernest Wilkinson in the early 1950s and 1960s. J. Golden Taylor, Thorton Y. Booth, Brigham Madsen, and Carlton Culmsee had all navigated to Logan after finding Provo inhospitable. They talked about academic freedom, or lack of it, continually. They blasted the LDS church in their daily classes. George Jensen, Austin Fife, Heber Snell, Venetta Nielsen, and Moyle Q. Rice were all great teachers, but they were harsh, sarcastic, and cynical so far as religious-sponsored education was concerned. Their collective delivery was precise and pointed.

George Jensen, a USU German professor, was given to making light of sacred things. Jensen, a returned Mormon missionary to Germany, became disaffected and as he aged evolved toward sacrilege. He loved to give sacred Mormon temple signs while shaking hands and say other things that upset students and faculty. Every so often, the board of trustees wanted him and others like him fired, but tenure provided protection. In his later years Jensen became worried that there might be truth in religion, so he promised after he died to come back and visit a younger colleague, Milton Abrams, in the event that it was true. Years later, Max Peterson rigged a speaker in the ceiling above Abrams's head and activated a tape that said simply, "Milton! It's true!" After that when Milton gave up coffee we decided to come clean in case he gave up smoking and came back to church.

In graduate school you were taught about tenure, academic freedom, and publish or perish. One of my professors had a memorable cartoon on his wall. The crucified Jesus and the two thieves were depicted in the background and one Roman soldier said, "They say he was a great teacher." The other responded, "Yeah, but did he publish?"

These incidents introduced me to the reality of campus life. There are always problems and difficult decisions, and a thorough analysis reveals that each institution creates its own criteria for retaining teachers. Parochial schools have clear statements about supportive and appropriate behavior.

In eight years' service as a department chair and eight more as an ombudsperson who oversaw due process in tenure and promotion meetings, I have seen a variety of challenges to academic freedom. My conclusion is that it is a treasure. It is also threatened. That is why its discussion has profound relevance. Public and private institutions have separate codes, presumably based on the guidelines of the American Association of University Professors (AAUP). However, there are numerous twists on the guidelines.

The educator W. T. Couch once wrote

> Academic Freedom is the principle designed to protect the teacher from hazards that tend to prevent (her) or him from meeting their obligations in the pursuit of truth. The obligations of the teacher are direct to truth, and the teacher who, in order to please anybody, suppresses important information, or says things he knows are not true, or refrains from saying things that need to be said in the interest of truth, betrays his calling and renders himself unworthy to belong in the company of teachers.

This is a solid and forthright opinion that deserves careful consideration.

Academic freedom as an idea is often considered more important than the ephemeral reality of particular people and circumstances. It is an idea that is gravely threatened in our time. Institutions with specific missions and goals can require unique behavior from their employees. That is not new. The maintenance of academic freedom also implies professional ethical standards of truthful disclosure and reasonable care. It is not nor has it ever been a blank check.

As First Amendment scholar William Van Alstyne points out, professors are protected in their "freedom" but not immune "from the power of others to use their authority to restrain its exercise." Universities or colleges are often faced with the reality of economic and curricular limitations. Consequently, an institution's decision not to offer a particular subject or not to provide financial means for a particular line of research may be faulted as educationally unenlightened, but such actions would not constitute an abridgment of freedom. However, freedom is abridged when sanctions are threatened against a faculty member because his or her interest pertains to a subject that the institution does not support. If an institution desires to be open and pluralistic, it must avoid any and all forms of censure. But in reality ultimate financial resources of almost all institutions of higher learning are beyond the control of the faculty. Only in rare cases do faculty manage resources.

Issues of professional integrity are resolved within a given institution. They are ultimately not overseen by extraneous professional groups issuing licenses. Insofar as public universities or colleges are concerned, the power to force hemlock on a modern Socrates is constrained, and private institutions generally adopt similar procedures as exist in public schools. The original body of oversight is usually a faculty or a faculty committee. Each campus generally has a mechanism whereby charges are filed and hearings are held. This is a well-tried process of peer evaluation. On issues of suspected infringement, an appeal process usually exists that allows a faculty member to seek help from the AAUP or from the administration.

Now let me personalize the discussion and bring it closer to home and to the reality that confronts this particular dialogue. That is to illustrate the difference between public and private institutions in Utah. On the surface, the process of academic freedom looks very similar; however, there are distinct differences.

On order from the State Board of Regents, Utah institutions have undergone a revision of faculty codes. The Utah State University faculty code states,

> The University is operated for the common good which depends upon the free search for truth and its free exposition. Academic Freedom is essential to these purposes and applies to teaching, research and service.
>
> The University is a community dedicated, through promulgation of thought, truth, and understanding, to teaching, research, and service. It must therefore be a place where innovative ideas, original experiments, creative activities, and independence of thought are not merely tolerated but actively encouraged. Because thought and understanding flourish only in a climate of intellectual freedom, and because the pursuit of truth is fundamentally a personal enterprise, a code statement of faculty responsibility must be strongly anchored to principles of intellectual freedom and personal autonomy. While faculty must abide by a code of standards of professional responsibility, the university must provide and safeguard a climate of intellectual freedom. Relationships within the university should consist of shared confidence, mutual loyalty,

and trust. Dealing should be conducted with courtesy, civility, decency, and a concern for personal dignity.

The code then elaborates:

Academic freedom is the right to teach, study, discuss, investigate, discover, create and publish freely. Academic freedom protects the rights of faculty members in teaching and of students in learning. Freedom in research is fundamental to the advancement of truth. The faculty member is entitled to full freedom in teaching, research, and creative activities, subject to the limitations imposed by professional responsibility.

Other institutions in the state and region vary. Westminster College has no tenure policy. It operates on three- or five-year renewable contracts. Community college professors are virtually unprotected in many respects. They do not have a national organization like AAUP. Untenured people at any institution clearly have problems. Frankly, private institutions can do what they want. President Rex Lee of BYU said there is more academic freedom at BYU than other universities because people can say positive things about their religion in the classroom.

Close examination of Brigham Young University's annual contract and code illustrates the abandonment of traditional academic freedom. In 1991 the contract was routine and said little about conduct and behavior; however, in 1992 the following statement was added:

Brigham Young University is a private university. It has unique goals and aspirations that arise from the mission of its sponsoring institution, The Church of Jesus Christ of Latter-day Saints. By accepting a contract of employment here, faculty members choose to accept, support, and participate in the University's religiously oriented educational mission, to observe and support the behavior standards of the University, including the Honor Code and Dress and Grooming Standards, and to further the University's objectives by being role models for a life that combines the quest for intellectual rigor with the quest for spiritual values and personal character. Faculty who are members of BYU's sponsoring Church also accept the spiritual and temporal expectations of wholehearted Church membership.

A year later an additional statement was included stipulating that faculty agree to "refrain from behavior or expression that seriously and adversely affects the University mission or the Church." In addition, "LDS faculty also accept as a condition of employment the standards of conduct consistent with qualifying for temple privileges."

The problem is that this policy takes continuance or tenure away from the hands of the university. If an ecclesiastical leader, a non-academic, revokes a professor's LDS temple recommend (which verifies personal worthiness in areas of belief and behavior), the individual can be terminated from employment.

If a person is terminated for not upholding the mission of a private institution or its sponsoring organization, that is legal. When such political termination is disguised in a charade of academic process, the school's honesty and morality are jeopardized. When a faculty member's academic ability is questioned for political, religious, or ideological issues, he or she has cause for redress, according to established academic protocol.

In reality, the problems of the Provo campus for LDS church headquarters in Salt Lake City have always existed. In the 1930s the Church Education System drove many talented instructors from their ranks over theological orthodoxy. Included in this group were Obert Tanner, Lynn Bennion, Daryl Chase, and Sterling McMurrin. BYU has always been willing to sacrifice professors and ideas in order to maintain theological orthodoxy. In this respect BYU is no different from any other parochial school which has been less than honest in its academic pretensions.

During the winter of Valley Forge, American revolutionary Tom Paine wrote, "These are the times that try men's souls." They are also the times that try women's souls. All concerned must understand the implied as well as written contract between scholars and their employers and the responsibility that accompanies freedom. Students are entitled to more than institutional insecurities about image and longevity. The human spirit deserves more leeway than short-sighted administrators sometimes allow. But they must if BYU is to fulfill a mission at all commensurate with the ideals of a university. And they will if they thoughtfully consider what is best for everyone involved.

9.
Religion and Academics at Brigham Young University: A Recent Historical Perspective

Gary James Bergera

Throughout its nearly 120-year history, Brigham Young University has tried to integrate religion and academics. Ranking church leaders who double as the school's board of trustees stress the importance of combining modern thought with religion, while at the same time pointing out obstacles. This balancing act, which weighs critical secularism with the non-rational world view of conservative religion, has fluctuated from shotgun marriage to uneasy truce and today serves as a microcosm of the LDS intellectual enterprise.

BYU's most consistent emphasis has been on demonstrating the rationality of Mormon beliefs. Two of the school's earliest research institutes were the Institute of Church Studies (1957) and the Institute of Mormon Studies (1964). The former was established to assist church authorities "in research and other problems"—which often meant compiling material for speeches; the latter was to provide the church with doctrinal studies. In 1965 a Book of Mormon Institute was founded, which produced motion pictures for use in the church's missionary program.[1] In 1976 BYU's religious institutes were consoli-

---

1. Ernest L. Wilkinson, ed., *Brigham Young University: The First One Hundred Years,* 4 vols. (Provo, UT: Brigham Young University Press, 1975-76),

dated into a single Center for Religious Studies. The center soon became known for its symposia and publications, which BYU philosopher Truman Madsen termed "real potboiler[s]" because of their ease in production and sales.[2]

Other campus research groups reflect similar interests. A Moral Studies group was organized in the 1970s under university president Dallin Oaks but was later dismantled when it became apparent that group members did not intend to publish their views for outside peer review. Similarly, the BYU Translation Sciences Institute had as its original goal development of simultaneous foreign translations of talks by church authorities. After ten years of discouraging results, the institute was relocated off campus as a more traditional and independent translation company. Other less-ambitious institutes with Mormon emphases have continued on campus, including the Center for Christian Values in Literature.[3]

4:378 (hereafter BYU); *Research Division Report*, 1971-72, 69, 79; 1972-73, 78, University Archives, Brigham Young University, Provo, Utah (hereafter BYUA).

    2. "Trustees OK Study Center," *Daily Universe*, 27 Feb. 1976; "Foreign Visitors to Lecture," *Daily Universe*, 13 Apr. 1977; "Book Review," *BYU Today*, Apr. 1979, 7; "Islam: Spiritual Foundations and Modern Manifestations," *Daily Universe*, 22 Oct. 1981; "Truman Madsen," *BYU Today*, Dec. 1981, 21-24. One of the books in the Religious Studies Center Monograph Series, *Book of Mormon Authorship: New Light on Ancient Origins*, edited by Noel B. Reynolds, has been characterized as "responsible apologetics" ("Responsible Apologetics," *Dialogue: A Journal of Mormon Thought* 16 [Winter 1983]: 140-44).

    3. "Behavior Institute Established at Y," *Daily Universe*, 29 Sept. 1976; "Philosophy Department Comes of Age," *Seventh East Press*, 10 June 1982); "In His Own Tongue," *Daily Universe*, 13 Oct. 1971. Harold B. Lee, first counselor in the LDS First Presidency, stated, "With our responsibility to teach the people of the world in fifty nations and in seventeen different languages, as we are now doing, think what it would mean to our missionary and teaching efforts if some scholars from this institution were to contribute to this possibility" by creating "some electronic device by which we could speak in English and our hearers could understand, each in his own language" ("Installation and Charge to the President," *Inaugural Addresses*,

In the classroom faculty and students have been encouraged, sometimes required, to modify curricula to reflect Mormon teachings. Apostle Harold B. Lee cautioned students in the late 1960s, "If you find in your school texts claims that contradict the word of the Lord, . . . you may be certain such teachings are but the theories of men."[4] "In all fields of secular learning," Apostle Delbert Stapley told BYU faculty, "if the text does not conform or agree with the teaching of the gospel then the scriptures and the teachings of God's oracles must supersede the speculations and opinions of men."[5] Founding law school dean Rex Lee added in 1973, "In those few instances in which the rational and the extrarational processes yield inconsistent results, it is the latter which must prevail."[6] In 1960 BYU trustees agreed to authorize a major in anthropology only on condition "that a member of the executive committee [counsel] with the teachers . . . before the program be put into effect."[7]

Two years earlier similar concern in another discipline had led to discontinuation of a philosophy class in existentialism.[8] One philosophy professor remembered, "There rarely was a semester that I did not have to defend myself and what I was teaching."[9] When in the mid-1960s philosophy faculty tried to inaugurate an open lecture series, the dean of the College of Religion noted that "Some of the [church] authorities have had some concern about

12 Nov. 1971, BYUA). "University Creates Corporation," *BYU Today,* June 1979, 8 (see also "Campus Chatter," *Seventh East Press,* 11 Aug. 1982); "Center for Study of Christian Values," *Daily Universe,* 28 Oct. 1980.

4. Harold B. Lee, *Youth and the Church* (Salt Lake City: Deseret Book Co., 1970), 192 (cf. "'Develop Testimony,' Pres. Lee Tells Youth," *Church News,* 6 May 1972).

5. Delbert L. Stapley, "Pre-School Faculty Address," Sept. 1970, 3, BYUA.

6. Harold B. Lee, "By Study and Also By Faith," in ASBYU Academics, *Best Lectures, 1973-74,* 71-72, BYUA (cf. "Learning Calls for Spirituality," *Daily Universe,* 15 May 1973).

7. Board of Trustees minutes, 4 Oct. 1961, BYUA.

8. Ibid., 14 Jan. 1959.

9. "BYU Students: Don't Read It If Not Righteous," *Daily Utah Chronicle,* 27 July 1983.

[even] offering philosophy [at BYU]."[10] The president agreed to the lectures on an "experimental basis, provided," he wrote, "[the faculty] can assure you that their sincere desire is to build testimonies of the truthfulness of the gospel rather than to raise questions and doubts in the minds of students or others who may attend."[11] A trustee stressed four years later that BYU's philosophy curriculum should be presented "in such a manner as to avoid the tendency of many academicians to measure their areas of discipline against the philosophy of the church."[12]

Such censorship has been evident in the management of the school's "voice for the community of LDS scholars," *Brigham Young University Studies*, where the consequences of displeasing trustees has been a recurring fear. Reviewing a submission entitled "LDS Scholar's Responsibility" in the late 1960s, one reader admitted that while he agreed with the author, he wondered what would happen if "one of the brethren disagreed with his position or with his procedure," thus "open[ing] up a series of controversies." Screening another essay, "The Growth and Development of the LDS Concept of God," a religion instructor thought "there would be some 'official' objection to the article as it now stands, even in the title, and both *Studies* and [the author] should be spared that experience." An essay on the church's health code would not "solve anything but just raise more issues and rationalizations," its two reviewers wrote, "stir[ring] up too much controversy in the minds of Latter-day Saint readers." A fourth article detailing church rituals would "draw heavy criticism from the brethren, and speaks of things that would be better left unpublished." Finally, an essay on an early Mormon apostate exhibited the wrong "tone":

> It seems to take an "objective" approach (i.e., I don't get the feeling the author is attacking Joseph Smith but at the same time he doesn't give us the impression that he does believe Joseph Smith was a prophet). It is not the purpose of *BYU Studies* to adopt

10. B. West Belnap to Earl C. Crockett, 3 Nov. 1964, BYUA.

11. Crockett to Belnap, 4 Nov. 1964, BYUA.

12. Boyd K. Packer, in Board of Trustees, Executive Committee minutes, 21 Nov. 1968, BYUA.

such an attitude. We should take it as a given that Joseph Smith was a true prophet. Therefore the paper cannot be published in *BYU Studies*.[13]

In 1973 the managing director of LDS public communications complained to BYU president Oaks that the findings of two BYU sociologists reflected negatively on the church.[14] The researchers had found that among practicing Mormons nearly 80 percent shop on Sunday, while only 8 percent would refuse an invitation to attend a movie on Sunday.[15] Oaks replied that "the distribution of scientific findings about how much active members of a church [deviate in behavior from church expectations] and yet maintain their self-concepts as active church members seems eminently proper." "Wherever possible," he explained, "our scholarly work should be made available for the benefit of the public, including our own members."[16] But three years later Oaks quashed release of a survey on stresses facing contemporary Mormon families. Reportedly, he was not convinced of several of the report's conclusions, notably that more LDS than non-LDS women in Utah work outside the home; that a mother's working outside the home does not have a negative effect on her family; and that the church may contribute to an increasing divorce rate among members by not providing adequate sex education for its youth.[17]

The academic treatment of sex has been one of the areas of greatest controversy at BYU. Since the early 1900s the school has

---

13. "Rejected Manuscripts," 1969, 1970, 1974, 1980, 1983, *Brigham Young University Studies*, Office Files, Brigham Young University.

14. Wendell J. Ashton to Dallin H. Oaks, 9 Nov. 1973, BYUA.

15. See Philip R. Kunz and Franklyn W. Dunford, "The Neutralization of Religious Dissonance," *Review of Religious Research*, Fall 1973, 2-9, cf. "Members Who Shop Sunday Have Guilt Feelings," *Daily Universe*, 4 Apr. 1973.

16. Oaks to Ashton, 20 Nov. 1973, BYUA.

17. "Notes of an interview with Boyd C. Rollins," 30 Jan. 1976, copy in private possession. Though the final report is unavailable, its major conclusions can be inferred from Rollins's "Annotated Bibliography on the Contemporary Mormon Family," 10 Apr. 1975.

offered an introductory course in sex education.[18] In 1953, President Ernest Wilkinson, alarmed at Alfred Kinsey's reports on sexual behavior, appointed a faculty committee to determine if the school's sex education provided a strong defense of chastity.[19] When members of the sociology department learned that the committee had decided "who shall teach [sex education] and where," they registered "strenuous objection to administrative prurience in this regard."[20] Wilkinson, however, knowing of "no more important need on our campus," pushed for a BYU-authored health textbook.[21] One of the school's faculty assigned to the project became skeptical that his treatment of sex could pass the scrutiny of both trustees and colleagues.[22] Some university administrators agreed, and the project was abandoned.[23] Instead, BYU officials arranged to have a national publisher remove objectionable material from a health text. When the publisher overlooked one offending page in 1967, BYU bookstore employees excised the page before placing the text on store shelves. Student reaction ranged from amusement to outrage.[24] Studies undertaken since have found that many freshmen enter BYU misinformed about sex, and that student attitudes towards sex education

---

18. BYU 1:484; "Overemphasized Morality," *Y News*, 14 Nov. 1930.

19. Alfred Kinsey et al., *Sexual Behavior in the Human Male* (Philadelphia: Saunders, 1948), and Alfred Kinsey et al., *Sexual Behavior in the Human Female* (Philadelphia: Saunders, 1953); Ernest L. Wilkinson to Antone K. Romney et al., 1 Oct. 1953, BYUA (cf. Committee on Sex Education minutes, 13 Oct. 1953, BYUA). At least two faculty committees were appointed to address the "Masturbation Problem" (Wilkinson to Romney et al.).

20. Sociology Faculty minutes, 11 Mar. 1955, BYUA.

21. See Board of Trustees, Executive Committee minutes, 1 Feb., 1 Mar. 1962; documents in UA 585, BYUA; Earl C. Crockett to Reed H. Bradford et al., 5 Apr. 1962, BYUA; Ernest L. Wilkinson to Milton F. Hartvigsen, 17 Dec. 1962, BYUA.

22. Henry J. Nicholes to Harvey L. Taylor, 20 Dec. 1962, 19 Feb. 1963, BYUA.

23. Henry L. Taylor to Ernest L. Wilkinson, 16 Apr. 1963, BYUA.

24. "Page Slashed From Text," *Daily Universe*, 25 Sept. 1967.

become more disapproving following enrollment in the university's required health classes.[25]

Administrators and faculty have also tried to referee Mormon teachings and secular theories on human personality development and psychotherapy. President Wilkinson felt that "any teacher who has to go to a psychiatrist . . . is not worthy of being on the BYU faculty,"[26] and the church's *Priesthood Bulletin* carried official caution against "studies or systems dealing with the complexities of the human personality."[27] Apostle Mark Petersen, in what he would term the "general attitude" of church authorities,[28] proclaimed that "our identity was fixed in the pre-existence even as it is preserved in the hereafter. It never has changed and never will change."[29] "The basic cause of mental and emotional illness," an assistant BYU professor of organizational behavior added two years later, "is disobedience to gospel law. . . . The Lord's approach to the world's sicknesses is to teach . . . faith, repentance, baptism, the Holy Ghost, [and] service."[30] A BYU psychologist promised, "There will be a Mormon

---

25. See Thomas L. Stinebaugh, "An Investigation of Health Misconceptions Among Students Enrolled in Personal Health Classes At Brigham Young University," M.S. thesis, Brigham Young University, 1974, 35-37 (cf. "Lack of Sex Education Lecturer's Topic," *Daily Universe*, 4 Feb. 1976); Erskine P. Ausbrooks III, "An Evaluation of Change in the Health Related Attitudes of Students Completing Personal Health 130 Instruction at Brigham Young University," M.S. thesis, Brigham Young University, 1975.

26. "Response of Ernest L. Wilkinson at Dinner Given For Himself and His Wife," 3 Aug. 1971, BYUA.

27. *Priesthood Bulletin* (Church of Jesus Christ of Latter-day Saints), Aug. 1972.

28. Inferred from Petersen to Gary J. Bergera, 13 May 1981 (see also Jack Jarrard, interview with Paul T Roberts, 8 June 1983, in Roberts, "A History of the Development and Objectives of the LDS *Church News* Section of the *Deseret News*," M.S. thesis, Brigham Young University, 1983, 61).

29. "Our Eternal Identity," *Church News*, 23 Mar. 1974.

30. Stephen R. Covey, in "Behavioral Science: Old Nemesis Looks for a New Roost," *BYU Today*, Mar. 1976, 1 (see also the response of Merritt H. Egan, a member of the American Psychiatric Association's National Task Force on Religion and Psychiatry).

applied behavioral science" that will "infuse scholarly work with values, revelations, and inspired methods of inquiry that derive from the gospel."[31]

Practical implementation of Mormon-based psychology proved difficult. Referring to the "blanket condemnation of certain kinds of therapy and group techniques [coming] from church leaders," BYU psychologist Mark Allen found that "these statements have been disturbing because they have not discriminated as to the legitimate and illegitimate uses" of such techniques.[32] In late 1969 BYU administrators announced they were curtailing the on-campus use of "electrical aversive therapy" except in treating homosexuality.[33] A Board of Review for Psychotherapeutic Techniques later identified eight therapies that conflicted with church teachings, including hypnosis, sensitivity training, and self-disclosure.[34]

In response to the increasing "personal problems of church members . . . in number and seriousness," together with the absence of "revealed truth about human behavior" among professionals "to combat these problems," President Oaks proposed to trustees in 1976 that "an Institute for Studies in Values and Human Behavior be established at BYU to sponsor and conduct research that would assist in preventing and changing behaviors which lead people away from eternal life." Trustees backed the appointment of BYU psychologist Allen Bergin as director.[35] Noting that "too many LDS behavioral scientists do not harmonize their professional concepts with their religious stands," Bergin explained that his "first project [would] be to state as clearly as possible to the behavioral

31. "Dr. Allen E. Bergin," *Century II*, Dec. 1976, 3; Allen E. Bergin, "Bringing the Restoration to the Academic World: Clinical Psychology as a Test Case," *Brigham Young University Studies*, Summer 1979, 449-73.

32. Mark K. Allen, "The History of Psychology at Brigham Young University," 156, BYUA.

33. Vice-Presidents' minutes, 22 Sept. 1969, BYUA (cf. "Professor 'Unconditions' Sneezing," *Alumnus*, Feb. 1969, 1).

34. David M. Sorenson to Members of the Board of Review for Psychotherapeutic Techniques, 5 Apr. 1976, BYUA.

35. Board of Trustees minutes, 1 Sept. 1976.

scientists . . . that Jesus Christ teaches in principles of behavior."[36] He later added, "What we can do is receive inspiration in our research and then seek reviews by the authorities [of the church] for their interpretations, disapproval, or whatever, if doctrinal questions are raised by it."[37] "Our basic theme," institute member Victor Brown, Jr., wrote, "is that truth lies with the scriptures and prophets, not with secular data or debate."[38]

The institute's primary assignment was to prepare a manuscript on homosexuality. "The church would fund the project," Oaks reported, "and the resulting book [would] be published by a press having nothing to do with the church in order to magnify its acceptability in the scholarly community and among non-church members."[39] Researchers were particularly proud of a 1978 doctoral dissertation, commissioned by the church's social services division, on the "Treatment of Homosexuality: A Reanalysis and Synthesis of Outcome Studies."[40] The study's conclusion that two-thirds of homosexuals seeking therapy reported some improvement was greeted by institute members as secular vindication of the church's position. Yet three years after the establishment of the institute, one member

---

36. Allen E. Bergin, in "Behavior Institute Established at Y," *Daily Universe*, 29 Sept. 1976.

37. "Bergin," *Century II*, 4 (cf. Allen E. Bergin, "Toward a Theory of Human Agency," *New Era*, Aug. 1973, 32-41).

38. Victor L. Brown, Jr., to Robert K. Thomas, 14 Nov. 1978, copy in private possession.

39. Related goals included "creation of a clinically oriented document in which sacred and secular data are gathered for guidance of parents, individuals, and curriculum writers"; an "LDS book on human behavior after the manner of *Articles of Faith*"; and "creation of a political action kit for use of member-citizens in local legislative efforts" (Dallin H. Oaks to Thomas S. Monson, 13 Sept. 1979, copy in private possession).

40. Elizabeth C. James, "Treatment of Homosexuality: A Reanalysis and Synthesis of Outcome Studies," Ph.D. diss., Brigham Young University, 1978 (Allen Bergin served as chair of James's doctoral committee). James reported that out of 101 published studies, 27 percent of subjects had "improved" and 37 percent had "recovered" with regards to their homosexuality.

admitted, "Sexuality is a risky business. Articles on the more general subject of mental health and values are much better investments."[41] By 1980 costs for the proposed defense of church teachings had reached close to $150,000, and some church authorities had become "squeamish" over the issue, while Bergin had concluded "that for him to complete [the] book under the conditions outlined (including direct church funding and the necessary review by persons representing the church) would seriously erode his professional standing ... and significantly reduce the desired impact of the book."[42] Bergin eventually bowed out of the project, and the completed work, a more general treatment of *Human Intimacy: Illusion and Reality*, published in 1981, listed Brown as its only author.[43] By the mid-1980s the institute had been dismantled and its remaining members assigned to other campus departments.

When the Department of Archaeology was founded in 1946, "the scope of the new department's interest ... was particularly directed towards research bearing on [Mormon] scriptures." Department chair Ross Christensen felt that "if our search nowhere turns up materials that can be fitted into the Book of Mormon picture of extensive civilizations of Near Eastern origin, then that record stands disproved."[44] Early expeditions into Central America "discovered important evidence bearing on the location of the Book of Mormon

---

41. Victor L. Brown, Jr., to Robert K. Thomas, 14 Nov. 1978, 11 Sept. 1979, copies in private possession.

42. Dallin H. Oaks to J. Richard Clarke, 7 Mar. 1979, copy in private possession.

43. Victor L. Brown, Jr., *Human Intimacy: Illusion and Reality* (Salt Lake City: Parliment Publishers, 1981), and Marvin Rytting's review in *Sunstone Review*, July 1982, 24ff.

44. Ross T. Christensen, "Why A Department of 'Archaeology'?" *The University Archaeological Society, Miscellaneous Papers, No. 19* (Provo, UT: n.p., Dec. 1960); *BYU Catalog*, 1 May 1946, 302-303; *BYU Catalog*, 1 May 1947, 107-10, and subsequent years. Christensen's recollections are found in the following essays from *Miscellaneous Papers, No. 19*: "On the Study of Archaeology by Latter-day Saints," 5, 9, 10; "Let George Do It," 17; "New Chairman Airs Views," 19; and "A Historical Sketch of the Department of Archaeology of Brigham Young University," 4 Mar. 1957, 36, BYUA.

cit[ies]."[45] Other trips followed, and with the inauguration in 1951 of an Annual Symposium on the Archaeology of the Scriptures sponsored by the University Archaeological Society (later Society for Early Historic Archaeology [SEHA]), Book of Mormon geography became an important topic on campus.[46] At one point, President Wilkinson bragged, "Our archaeology is taught clearly from a Book of Mormon standpoint."[47]

As naivete and overzealousness became apparent,[48] however, a 1959 proposal for "a large excavation program in Central America to verify the Book of Mormon" failed to receive administrative approval. Officials were convinced that some research had been "so biased that they will not stand the test of objective archaeological conclusions." Thus "if we are to do further excavating," administrators decided, "it should be done largely by non-Mormons who will merely give a description of what they find, leaving the world to make conclusions."[49] As a result, the New World Archaeological Foundation (NWAF), creation of a California attorney in 1952 and church-funded since 1955, was instructed to "concern itself only with the culture history interpretations normally within the scope of archaeology, and any attempt at correlation or interpretation involving the Book of Mormon should be eschewed."[50] "I welcomed the instruction as

45. "Archaeologists Explore Probable City Bountiful," *Daily Universe*, 3 Mar. 1961; Michael Coe, "Mormons and Archaeology: An Outside View," *Dialogue: A Journal of Mormon Thought* 6 (Autumn 1973): 44

46. See Joseph E. Vincent, "Some Views on Book of Mormon Geography," and C. Stuart Bagley, "A New Approach to the Geography of the Book of Mormon," in Forrest R. Hauck, ed., *Papers of the Fourteenth Annual Symposium on the Archaeology of the Scriptures* (Provo, UT: Department of Extension Publications, 1963), 61-86.

47. Ernest L. Wilkinson to J. Elliot Cameron, 20 Nov. 1968, BYUA.

48. See Dee F. Green, "Book of Mormon Archaeology: The Myths and the Alternatives," *Dialogue: A Journal of Mormon Thought*, Summer 1969, 76-77.

49. Ernest L. Wilkinson journal, 22 Aug. 1959, photocopy, Wilkinson Collection, Special Collections, Marriott Library, University of Utah, Salt Lake City.

50. Fred W. Nelson, "Thomas Stuart Ferguson, 1915-83," 22

refreshing after my earlier days at BYU," wrote a former NWAF archaeologist in 1969, "when everything the archaeology department did had to be 'scripturally' related."[51] NWAF-sponsored expeditions have since excavated at the Cinco Pisos pyramid in the Edzna valley, Campeche, Mexico, and the ruins of El Mirador, Guatemala.[52] In addition, New World explorations in Chiapas, Mexico, "have put that state on the archaeological map and have established one of the longest and best archaeological sequences for any part of the" Americas.[53] Following persistent insinuations that NWAF's ties to the LDS church prevented its employees from reaching "scientific" conclusions, it was reorganized in mid-1976 as a "separately identified but subsidiary entity" of BYU.[54]

Some BYU faculty have continued the task of proving Book of Mormon claims. John L. Sorenson, archaeology chair, assembled an elaborate map of Book of Mormon cities tied to mesoamerican ruins.[55] And more recently the Foundation for Ancient Research and

---

Oct. 1983, 11, 14, privately circulated; Wilkinson journal, 22 Aug. 1959. For Ferguson's later reversal on Book of Mormon historicity, see Stan Larson, "The Odyssey of Thomas Stuart Ferguson," *Dialogue: A Journal of Mormon Thought*, Spring 1990, 55-93.

51. Green.

52. See "BYU Group Explores in Yucatan," *Daily Universe*, 2 Mar. 1973; "Archaeology Team Begins Excavation of Mayan City," *BYU Today*, Mar. 1979, 1; "Y Archaeologists Working in Guatamala," *Daily Universe*, 20 Oct. 1980; "Dig Uncovers Mayan Origins," *BYU Today*, Mar. 1983, 35; *A Quarter of a Century in Mexico* (Provo, UT: New World Archaeological Foundation, 1978).

53. Coe.

54. Leo P. Vernon to Dallin H. Oaks, 22 Apr. 1976, with attachment, copy in private possession; Board of Trustees Minutes, 2 June 1976; Oaks to Howard W. Hunter, 27 July 1976, and First Presidency to Oaks, 30 July 1976, copies in private possession. See also BYU 3:120-25.

55. "FARMS Tours: Here We Go Again," *Insights: An Ancient Window*, Oct. 1984; John L. Sorenson, "Digging Into the Book of Mormon," 6, 7, 13, copy in private possession, published, with some changes, as "Digging Into the Book of Mormon: Our Changing Understanding of Ancient America and Its Scripture," *Ensign*, Sept. 1984, 26-37, and Oct. 1984, 12-23. Sorenson's

Mormon Studies (FARMS), an offshoot of SEHA and NWAF, has produced a growing collection of inter-disciplinary defenses of Book of Mormon historicity based on Sorenson's speculations. Guided tours of ruins, conducted by Sorenson, began in early 1984, and were followed by classes in Book of Mormon archaeology in the anthropology department.[56] But archaeological proofs remain elusive. Sorenson's own manuscript was rejected for publication by BYU's Religious Studies Center because Apostle Mark Petersen found the topic "too touchy."[57] Only after Petersen's death in 1984 did FARMS and church-owned Deseret Book jointly publish Sorenson's and other related works.[58]

Equally problematic in accommodating a curriculum of religion and academics has been the writing of Mormon history. "Until the past twenty-five years," observed non-LDS historian Lawrence Foster in 1982, "the very idea of Mormon history [was] viewed as a joke by most professional historians."[59] In the 1930s BYU professor

---

theories are most fully stated in *An Ancient American Setting for the Book of Mormon* (Salt Lake City: Deseret Book Co., 1985).

56. The Society for Early Historic Archaeology announced its own courses in scriptural archaeology. For cautionary statements, see Martin Raish, "All That Glitters: Uncovering Fool's Gold in Book of Mormon Archaeology," *Sunstone*, Jan./Feb. 1980, 10-15, and Raymond T. Matheny, remarks delivered during the Sixth Annual Sunstone Theological Symposium, 25 Aug. 1984. *Insights: An Ancient Window*, Mar. 1984.

57. Religious Instruction Administrative Council minutes, 31 May 1978, BYUA (cf. 27 July 1978: "Elder Petersen said it should not be published by our center").

58. "An Ancient American Setting for the Book of Mormon," *Insights: An Ancient Window*, Oct. 1984; "Volunteers Team Up to Study Book of Mormon," *BYU Today*, Feb. 1985, 15-16.

59. Lawrence Foster, "New Perspectives on the Mormon Past," *Sunstone*, Jan./Feb. 1982, 41. For useful surveys of Mormon historiography, see Howard C. Searle, "Early Mormon Historiography: Writing the History of the Mormons, 1830-1858," Ph.D. diss., University of California, Los Angeles, 1979; Clara Viator Dobay, "Essays in Mormon Historiography," Ph.D. diss., University of Houston, 1980; LeAnn Cragun, "Mormons and History: In Control of the Past," Ph.D. diss., University of Hawaii, 1981; and

Wilford Poulson pursued his studies of early church history in secret, fearing repercussions if school or church leaders learned of his activities.[60] By the 1950s an increasing number of professionally trained Mormon historians had begun meeting informally to share research findings and "stratagems by which [they] could overcome the reluctance of [church administrators] to allow [them] access to the rich materials housed [in church archives]."[61] Budding historians were "taken aback" when an article on Mormon health practices by Leonard J. Arrington, published in the inaugural issue of *BYU Studies*, aroused "such an opposition on the part of one zealous [church] authority that the journal was suspended for a year."[62] The director of BYU libraries later admitted to President Wilkinson, "The idea that anything controversial involving the church will not be given fair treatment or will not be made available for publication at Brigham Young University . . . is a problem we are continually faced with."[63]

Despite such obstacles,[64] interest in LDS history snowballed. In 1965 the Mormon History Association was organized. Seven years

Thomas G. Alexander, "Toward the New Mormon History: An Examination of the Literature on the Latter-day Saints in the Far West," in Michael P. Malone, ed., *Historians and the American West* (Lincoln: University of Nebraska Press, 1983), 344-68.

60. Samuel W. Taylor, *Rocky Mountain Empire* (New York: Macmillan, 1978), 225, 231-35.

61. Leonard J. Arrington, "Reflections on the Founding and Purpose of the Mormon History Association, 1965-1983," *Journal of Mormon History*, 1983, 91, 92.

62. Arrington, "Reflections," 91, 92, and, "An Economic Interpretation of the Word of Wisdom," *Brigham Young University Studies*, Winter 1959, 37-49.

63. S. Lyman Tyler to Ernest L. Wilkinson, 19 Apr. 1962, BYUA.

64. For examples of some of the criticisms leveled at Mormon historians during the mid- to late-1960s, see Ernest L. Wilkinson to Daniel H. Ludlow, 19 Feb. 1968, BYUA; LaMar Berrett, "A Statement Concerning Leonard J. Arrington," 1968, BYUA; Dean R. Zimmerman to Whom It May Concern, 1968, BYUA (cf. Daniel H. Ludlow to Ernest L. Wilkinson, 27 Dec. 1968, BYUA).

later Leonard Arrington was officially appointed Church Historian in 1972, a position formerly reserved for church authorities. "Now [the Church Historian's office] is going to be a dispenser of information, and I thoroughly approve of the new policy," commented retired BYU president Wilkinson.[65] "It was," an assistant to Arrington later wrote, "a golden decade—that someone has likened to Camelot."[66] Arrington and his staff inaugurated a sixteen-volume sesquicentennial history of the church and a Mormon Heritage series of edited documents, discovered and cataloged more than fifty boxes of previously unknown historical materials, assisted church archivists in the preparation of registers and guides to archival collections, initiated an oral history program, established a summer fellowship for graduate students, and produced an impressive array of task papers, articles, monographs, and books.[67]

Arrington's philosophy of history helped spawn what has been called the New Mormon History. As defined by BYU historian Thomas Alexander, it "derived from a belief that secular and spiritual motivation coexist in human affairs and that a sympathetic but critical evaluation of the Mormon past, using techniques derived from historical, humanistic, social-scientific, and religious perspectives, could help in understanding what was at base a religious movement."[68] Under Arrington's and others' direction, "a sense of excitement and exhilaration was generated as increasing numbers of Latter-day Saints began to develop a direct, personal sense of their own history, [and] a deeper appreciation of the richness and complexity of the Mormon past."[69]

---

65. Wilkinson journal, 19 Sept. 1972.

66. Davis Bitton, "Ten Years in Camelot: A Personal Memoir," *Dialogue: A Journal of Mormon Thought*, Autumn 1983, 9.

67. Ibid.

68. Alexander, "Toward the New Mormon History," 344. See also David Whittaker's review essay, "Historians and the Mormon Experience: A Sesquicentennial Perspective," *A Sesquicentennial Look at Church History—The Eighth Annual Sidney B. Sperry Symposium* (Provo, UT: BYU Religious Instruction, 1980), 293-327.

69. Foster, "New Perspectives," 42.

Support for New Mormon History proved shortlived. Church authorities expressed concern in 1974 when a director of the LDS Institute of Religion adjacent to the University of Utah publicly detailed connections between Mormonism and Freemasonry.[70] Less than two years later Ezra Taft Benson, president of the Quorum of Twelve Apostles, denounced "revisionist" historians whose "purpose has been and is to create a 'new history.'" "The emphasis," he declared, "is to underplay revelation and God's intervention in significant events, and to inordinately humanize the prophets of God so that their human frailties become more apparent than their spiritual qualities. . . . No writer can accurately portray a prophet of God if he or she does not believe in prophecy."[71] Benson later specifically warned teachers about interpreting church history. To say, he explained,

> that the Word of Wisdom [the Mormon health code] was an outgrowth of the temperance movement in America and that Joseph Smith selected certain prohibitions and dietary features from that movement and presented them to the Lord for confirmation is also to pronounce an explanation contradictory to the one given by Brigham Young. To suggest that Joseph Smith received the vision on the three degrees of glory . . . as he grappled for answers that contemporary philosophers were grappling for, is to infer an interpretation contrary to the prophet's own.

"Avoid expressions and terminology which offend the brethren and church members," Benson continued, insisting that "A revelation of God is not an experiment."[72]

The impact at BYU was apparent. The next year religion administrators ruled that an instructor "should choose another topic instead of talking on polygamy [for a spring faculty lecture] for the problems

---

70. See Richard Stephen Marshall, "The New Mormon History," Senior Honors Project, University of Utah, 1 May 1977, 51-56.

71. Ezra Taft Benson, "God's Hand in Our Nation's History," 28 Mar. 1976, 4, 9, BYUA (cf. "Fireside Theme: God Shaped Past," *Daily Universe*, 30 Mar. 1976).

72. Ezra Taft Benson, "The Gospel Teacher and His Message," 17 Sept. 1976, 15-16, BYUA.

it could cause."[73] In 1978, at the request of Apostle Petersen, an investigation was conducted of a BYU undergraduate and his teacher when the student wrote a paper analyzing the church's 1890 Manifesto banning polygamy.[74]

By 1980 LDS authorities had decided to "scuttle the sixteen-volume [sesquicentennial] history," to "circumscribe [other] projects that [had been] approved," to "reject any suggestions, however meritorious, for worthy long-range projects," to "allow the [Church Historical Department] to shrink by attrition," and to limit access to important collections in church archives.[75] Plans for a BYU-sponsored church history symposium were modified. Trustees ruled that "no extensive advertising should be made . . . and any publication should not be announced in advance but should be determined following the outcome of a careful review after the symposium."[76] Arrington and the majority of his colleagues were transferred to BYU as the newly formed Joseph Fielding Smith Institute for Church History, away from church archives and contact with church officials.[77]

---

73. Religious Instruction Administrative Council minutes, 8 Dec. 1977, BYUA.

74. David John Buerger, "Politics and Inspiration: An Historical Analysis of the Woodruff Manifesto," 10 Aug. 1978; Mark E. Petersen to Gregory E. Austin, 8 Sept. 1978 (cf. Petersen to Gordon B. Hinckley, 8 Sept. 1978); Buerger to Austin, 17 Sept. 1978; Dallin H. Oaks to Hinckley, 29 Sept. 1978; copies in private possession.

75. Bitton, "Ten Years," 18-19 (cf. "Campus Chatter," *Seventh East Press*, 28 Sept. 1982, and "Church Takes Active Interest in Books," *Seventh East Press*, 8 Mar. 1983); "Church Archives Restrict Access to General Authority Documents," *Seventh East Press*, 14 Mar. 1982; "Access to Church Archives: Penetrating the Silence," *Sunstone Review*, Sept./Oct. 1983, 4-7; "Church Historian: Evolution of a Calling," *Sunstone*, Apr. 1985, 46-48.

76. Board of Trustees, Executive Committee minutes, 24 June 1980 (cf. Ellis T. Rasmussen to Dallin H. Oaks, 13 June 1980, in private possession).

77. "Church Department Joins Y," *Daily Universe*, 3 July 1980 (cf. Cragun, "Mormons and History," 303-306). Smith Institute employees later posted the following sign on their bulletin board: "History is on our

"The Lord made it very clear that some things are to be taught selectively, and some things are to be given only to those who are worthy," Elder Boyd Packer warned in August 1981. "One who chooses to follow the tenets of his profession, regardless of how they may injure the church or destroy the faith of those not ready for 'advanced history' is himself in spiritual jeopardy."[78] Soon afterwards Arrington was formally notified that he was no longer Church Historian.

Among the first to hazard a public response to criticisms of their profession was D. Michael Quinn, BYU associate professor of history. Speaking to BYU history majors in November 1981, Quinn commented that the kind of church history required by Benson and Packer bordered on "idolatry." He explained:

> If a Latter-day Saint historian discussed the revelation to Joseph Smith about abstinence from tobacco, strong drinks, and hot drinks, and then failed to note that during the 1830s religious reformers and social reformers were involved nationally in urging abstinence from the identical things, any reader would have cause to criticize the historian and doubt his motives as well as his affirmation of the revelation's truth. . . . Mormon historians would be false to their understanding of LDS doctrine, Sacred History of the scriptures, the realities of human conduct, and documentary evidence if they sought to defend the proposition that LDS prophets were infallible in their decisions and statements.[79]

---

side . . . as long as we can control the historians" ("Campus Chatter," *Seventh East Press*, 7 Nov. 1982).

78. Boyd K. Packer, "The Mantle Is Far, Far Greater Than the Intellect," 22 Aug. 1981, typescript, 9, 11, 15 (also in *Brigham Young University Studies*, Summer 1981, 259-79). See also Packer, "Keeping Confidences," *Church Employees Lecture Series*, 18 Jan. 1980.

79. Quinn, "On Being A Mormon Historian," Nov. 1981, 16, 17, 9, 14, privately circulated (cf. "Historian Responds to Apostle," *Seventh East Press*, 18 Nov. 1981). Quinn revised his speech for *Sunstone* magazine but was dissuaded from publication by a number of supporters. It was published more than a decade later in George D. Smith, ed., *Faithful History: Essays on Writing Mormon History* (Salt Lake City: Signature Books, 1982).

Quinn was quietly reprimanded for his comments, and his research was curtailed. He would later resign from BYU citing university-imposed restrictions on writing as his primary reason.

While some BYU faculty found this anti-intellectual posturing distressing, others sided with the critics of Mormon historians. A professor of political science wrote,

> It is depressing to see some historians now struggling to get on the stage to act out the role of the mature, honest historian committed to something called "objective history," and, at the same time, the role of the faithful Saint. The discordance between those roles has produced more than a little bad faith (that is, self-deception) and even, perhaps, some blatant hypocrisy; it has also produced some pretentious, bad history.[80]

Apostle Bruce McConkie voiced disdain for "wise and learned" scholars, whose writings "twist and pervert the scriptures to conform to their traditions, and if they get anything right it is an accident."[81] "No Latter-day Saint who is true and faithful in all things," he later added, "will ever pursue a course, or espouse a cause, or publish an article or book that weakens or destroys faith."[82]

Eventually belief alone would prove reason enough to dismiss a teacher when BYU decided in 1988 to terminate the employ of David Wright, assistant professor of Asian and Near Eastern languages. Wright was told that his personal views on the Book of Mormon, biblical prophecy, and scriptural historicity—which administrators admitted he had not taught on campus—"differ so significantly from those generally accepted" by the LDS church that "we cannot con-

---

80. Louis Midgley, "A Critique of Mormon Historians: The Question of Faith and History," 30 Sept. 1981, 53-55, copy in private possession. See also Midgley's "call to arms" in "Some Challenges to the Foundations," an address delivered to members of the faculty of Religious Instruction, 14 Sept. 1984, copy in private possession.

81. Bruce R. McConkie, "The Bible—A Sealed Book," 17 Aug. 1984, 8-9, 11, copy in private possession, cf. McConkie, "The Doctrinal Restoration," 3 Nov. 1984, copy in private possession.

82. Bruce R. McConkie, "The Caravan Moves On," *Ensign*, Nov. 1984, 84.

tinue your employment."[83] Feminist scholars have likewise been criticized for their professional and extracurricular activities. "My biggest concern about the radical feminist critique," BYU's provost Bruce Hafen announced in 1993, "is its potential to undermine religious faith when it rejects hierarchical and patriarchal institutions to the point of rejecting scripture, priesthood authority, and prophets. My biggest problem . . . is not that it favors women, but that it can disfavor divine revelation."[84]

As BYU's checkered history indicates, secular education and religious instruction are rarely compatible. As BYU alumnus and former University of Oregon president Meredith Wilson wrote, "The tensions between a vigorous church and a vigorous university are greater than many may suppose."[85] The "BYU problem," noted Bruce Hafen, consists of "educational excellence juxtaposed with, and often colliding against, our concern for spiritual excellence."[86] President Oaks remarked at his 1980 farewell that when scholarship and religion are blended, the university runs the "significant risk that our efforts to end the separation between scientific scholarship and religion will merely produce a substandard level of performance, where religion dilutes scholarship instead of enlightening it, or where scholarship replaces religion instead of extending its impact. . . . A genuine mingling of the insights of reason and revelation," he confessed, "is infinitely . . . difficult."[87]

---

83. Jae R. Ballif to David P. Wright, 13 June 1988; David P. Wright, "Re: My Termination at Brigham Young University," 21 July 1988; copies of both in private possession. See also "BYU Professor Terminated for Book of Mormon Beliefs," *Sunstone*, May 1988, 43-44.

84. Bruce C. Hafen, "'Teach Ye Diligently and My Grace Shall Attend You,'" *1993 Pre-School Faculty Workshop Addresses* (Provo, UT: Brigham Young University, 1993), 9.

85. O. Meredith Wilson to Ronald L. Priddis and Gary J. Bergera, 21 Mar. 1985.

86. Bruce R. Hafen, "Reflections on Being at BYU," *Best Lectures, 1973-74* (ASBYU Academics), 41.

87. Dallin H. Oaks, "Challenge to BYU in the Eighties," BYU Commencement Address, 15 Aug. 1980, 16-17, BYUA.

Recurring conflicts at BYU point to a problem that has no apparent solution. Research has consistently indicated that "religion and scholarship tend to be incompatible."[88] While LDS church and BYU officials would no doubt like to believe that their school is immune,[89] they will eventually have to chose one or the other.[90]

---

88. See Stephen Steinberg, "Religious Involvement and Scholarly Productivity Among American Academics," in Martin Trow, ed., *Teachers and Students; Aspects of American Higher Education* (New York: McGraw-Hill, 1975), 85-112; and David Caplovitz and Fred Sherrow, *The Religious Drop-Outs: Apostasy Among College Graduates* (Beverly Hills: Sage Productions, 1977).

89. See Rex E. Lee, "Inaugural Response," *Address Delivered at the Inauguration of President Rex Edwin Lee, Brigham Young University, Provo, Utah, October 27, 1989,* 9. Several studies have reported a positive correlation between education and religiosity among Mormons. See Correlation Evaluation, "Religious Activity Among Latter-day Saints," Feb. 1982, copy in private possession; Stott, "Effects of College Education"; and esp. Stan L. Albrecht and Tim Heaton, "Secularization, Higher Education, and Religiosity," *Review of Religious Research*, Sept. 1984, 43-58. As Albrecht and Heaton have admitted, however, these studies may be flawed by respondent bias in favor of "active" Mormons and do not test for the following: the secularizing effects of specific college majors, the direction of religiosity while in college, variables after college that may mitigate the secularizing effects of education, and the effects of highly secularized universities on Mormon students. Cf. Marsden, "Campus Religious Group Participation;" Clifton Amundsen and Gary E. Madsen, "A Comparison of Mormons and Non-Mormon Faculty Religiosity," *Measuring Mormonism*, Fall 1977, 54-64; and Ray E. Paskett, "The Differential Effects of Bases for Moral Behavior and Major Field of Study Upon Moral Judgment," M.S. thesis, Brigham Young University, 1960.

90. The national honor society Phi Beta Kappa recognizes this and has consistently refused to charter a BYU chapter. See "Phi Beta Kappa Rejects BYU Chapter Again," *Salt Lake Tribune*, 20 May 1992, B-1.

Part III
Feminism

10.
A Feminist Comparison
of Mormonism
and Humanism

Bonnie Bullough

Mormonism had its origin in early nineteenth-century western New York, a frontier that still welcomed new ideas, including experimentation and challenges to traditional gender norms. John Humphrey Noyes argued male-female duality of the Godhead in his utopia in Oneida. Seneca Falls hosted the first women's rights meeting in 1848. Nearby was the futuristic community of Harmony, Pennsylvania, with its egalitarian ideas.

Several religions originated in the area at about the same time: Christian Science, Spiritualism, Seventh Day Adventism, and Mormonism. The Disciples of Christ (sometimes called Campbellites) were established in nearby Pennsylvania and Ohio. All shared the enthusiasm that accompanies a new religion, and all were different from traditional Protestantism. Mormonism, Seventh Day Adventism, and Christian Science included dietary restrictions, and preached a gospel of good health. Several of the religions were messianic, and all viewed God in a more personal way than traditional Christianity.

Women were emerging as spiritual guides: Mary Baker Eddy was a leader of Christian Science; Mother White was important in Seventh Day Adventism; and several well-known Spiritualists were women. Mormon men and women were not unaffected by such ideas, and for a time women held leadership positions in the church. Eliza Snow emphasized God the Mother, and Emma Smith, the wife of Joseph

Smith, was outspoken on matters of policy. After the death of her husband Emma left the Mormon church in a power struggle with Brigham Young and helped establish the Reorganized LDS church. Mormonism developed a conservative stance and looked back to the paternalism and authority of ancient Israel—emphasizing Jehovah, the God of Abraham, Isaac, and Moses. They supported plural marriage, male priesthood, male leadership, and repression of women. Women were recognized for the support they gave men, rather than for their own accomplishments.

Although historians of humanism trace its origins to the fifteenth century, humanism did not develop as an organized social movement until the twentieth century when it was established as an arm of the Unitarian church. Edmund Wilson, minister of the Salt Lake City Unitarian church, was a founder and leader of humanist thought in the 1940s and 1950s. Humanism has now spread back to Europe, with a total of ninety organizations belonging to the International Humanist and Ethical Union. There are significant contingents in the Netherlands, Norway, and Germany where people are required to designate a church for their state contributions and many people prefer humanism to traditional churches.

Some call humanism a religion and some do not. It is a system of beliefs which accepts all of the great philosophers as wise, but none has the last word because the search for truth is eternal. Probably the favorite philosophers of humanism are the great rationalists: Descartes, Spinoza, Locke, Voltaire, and Dewey. Robert Ingersoll is also respected for his work in the atheist movement. A belief in rationalism naturally led to support of the scientific method, so modern science is promoted, although science is thought of as blind to questions of morality, the ethics of philosophy are needed to shape the moral directions of humanism. None of these philosophies was particularly repressive of women, but the great philosophers and spokesmen were men. Women as people and as a class were somewhat outside the domain and concern of the philosophies, except insofar as they were linked under the generic term "man."

Although humanism was organized in the twentieth century, the philosophers it honors are from the eighteenth and nineteenth centuries. Current humanist writers often look back to a nineteenth century culture, so in many ways Mormonism and humanism share the same cultural heritage built on a paternalistic Judeao-Christian base. Women in that culture had very little status and they filled roles subservient to men. The two sexes were also segregated. This cultural heritage can be seen in the Mormon church, with the separation of the male priesthood and the female Relief Society. Women are not allowed to be bishops, stake presidents, general authorities, or fill any of the other decision-making offices in the church.

Women work and are fully accepted within the organizational structure of humanism and have held all major offices. Even though they are as likely to fill as important offices as men, they have not been philosophers of the movement. The great thinkers and writers of the movement remain mostly men; and since it is primarily a movement of ideas rather than activities, this is important. This may well be due to the fact that women did not get degrees in philosophy until recently, but some humanist women still feel deprived when they realize that most of the discourse is by men, about men, and quoting men. A women's caucus was established at the last international meeting of humanists, which was held in Berlin in summer of 1993. Thus the Humanist Women's caucus and the philosophers are corollaries to the Mormon Relief Society and the priesthood.

Probably Mormonism and humanism differ most on the issue of authority. Mormons believe there is a god who rewards and punishes, and that god is male. More significant is the fact that the president of the Mormon church speaks for God, and God's pronouncements in the last two decades have been paternalistic and repressive of women. In this regard the president of the Mormon church is congruent with the pope of the Catholic church who has indicated that God is against all mechanical and chemical birth control methods and considers the fetus to be a complete human being at the moment of conception, so abortion is never possible. In addition, God as interpreted by the Mormon hierarchy was apparently against the Equal Rights Amendment, an issue which the pope has not yet addressed.

Most Protestant churches, with the exception of a few fundamentalist cults, do not believe in a current living representative of God on earth. Most Hindus and Buddhists lack a living prophet; Confucianism is purely philosophical. Only one sect of Islam, Shiite Muslims, see their mullahs as God's agents. All other Muslims look back to the prophet Mohammed. Churches which accept current divine spokesmen allow members less freedom of conscience to decide what is right and wrong.

A living prophet has awesome authority and presents an almost insurmountable barrier to change. There is an extra added burden borne by Mormon and Shiite Muslim women because the prophet and the word of God are so near. The pope is more remote, not only in distance from America, but in style. Consequently the majority of eligible American Catholic women use birth control.

Humanists do not accept divine authority, arguing instead that people need to attend to making the world a better place or it will not improve. They do not believe in an after-life, heaven and hell, divine punishment, or divine rewards. Women are as devoid of the divine support system as men, so they are at the most basic level equal.

In spite of traditional religious prohibitions, a women's movement has again appeared and reached into Mormonism. The current movement is in fact a second wave, with the first phase occurring late in the nineteenth century and early in the twentieth, and culminating with American women achieving the vote, which Mormon activists also championed. After that triumph, women relaxed and moved back to the kitchen, losing some of the gains they had realized. Betty Friedan, a humanist, identified women's post-war attitude as the "feminine mystique." The second wave can be dated from the publication of her 1965 book. While we can credit her with issuing the rallying cry, probably the most important factor in the present movement was the new reproductive freedom occasioned by oral contraceptives in 1960, changes in law to allow their distribution, and revised abortion laws which culminated in the U.S. Supreme Court decision in Roe v. Wade in 1973.

Being able to time and control reproduction gave women a freedom they had never before experienced and opened up significant possibilities for women to move ahead in the occupational structure and have more sexual freedom, educational opportunities, and the possibility of being elected or appointed to public office. Moreover, it looks as if many of these changes will be permanent.

There is, however, a backlash typified by the "right-to-life" movement. It has occurred partly because men have realized the significance of changes and fear women will lose their subservience. Mormon men, including church authorities, have supported the backlash and used the Equal Rights Amendment and abortion issues to focus their attacks. Humanist men have generally supported the second wave of feminism, although only a handful of them have been in the forefront of the battle.

The backlash has had another unfortunate consequence. Fundamentalist leaders of the "right-to-life" movement have broadened their focus from abortion to birth control, so family planning has become more of a sin than it was in an earlier era. Another trend which has accompanied the women's movement has been an increase in the number of households headed by women, which usually means households plagued by poverty. Poverty has become a way of life for a large segment of our population, and those families tend to be headed by women. In the case of Mormon women a high rate of out-of-wedlock pregnancies has resulted in early marriages which are often unstable.

Some Mormon women have lost the love and support of men who are threatened by women's drive for freedom. Many have been punished for participating in the women's movement. Mormon ERA activist Sonia Johnson was an early victim of this repression and was excommunicated (see her *From Housewife to Heretic* [Garden City, NY, 1981]). Her ideas did not die, and there are an increasing number of Mormon women who are speaking out for women's rights. Some of them do historical research and find that women have lost power from the early church to the present time. They too are being excommunicated for their research and writing on this topic, but their ideas will not die. They are a force that the LDS church will eventually deal with if it is to stay viable in the twenty-first century.

So how do the positions of Mormon and humanist women compare? We share roots in the nineteenth-century Judeao-Christian male culture, but the lack of divine authority gives humanist women more freedom. Humanist men like to be taken care of by devoted wives, just like Mormon men; they continue to focus on great rational philosophers of the past, when paternalism reigned supreme, but they do not have the power of God to back them up. The more favorable position of humanist women leaves us with less motivation for change. We can, however, take inspiration from our Mormon sisters. The women's movement has come to Mormonism thirty years after it came to most Americans, but it has come at a critical time when the reactionary backlash threatens to obliterate progress. Mormon women now orchestrate a vigorous, thoughtful movement with determined leadership whose martyrdom will not stop the reform.

11.
The Struggle to Emerge: Leaving Brigham Young University

Martha Sonntag Bradley

British writer Virginia Woolf spoke in 1931 before a group of women who had been barred from entrance into male-dominated professions. She acknowledged their grievances, even their pain, and then suggested they might try writing as a career, saying that there were no legal obstacles to succeed at writing, only barriers one created for oneself. She said:

> While I was writing [this] review I discovered that if I were going to review books I should need to do battle with a certain phantom. And the phantom was a woman, and when I came to know her better I called her after the heroine of the famous poem, "The Angel of the House." It was she who used to come between me and my paper when I was writing reviews. It was she who bothered me and wasted my time and so tormented me that at last I killed her. . . .
>
> [W]hen I came to write I encountered her with the very first words. The shadow of her wings fell on my page; I heard the rustling of her skirts in the room. Directly, that is to say, I took my pen in my hand to review that novel by a famous man, she slipped behind me and whispered, "My dear, you are a young woman. You are writing about a book that has been written by a man. Be sympathetic; be tender; flatter; deceive; use all the arts and wiles of our sex. Never let anybody guess that you have a mind of your own. Above all, be pure." And she made as if to guide my pen ....

> Had I not killed her she would have killed me. She would have plucked the heart out of my writing. . . . Thus whenever I felt the shadow of her wing or the radiance of her halo upon my page, I took up the inkpot and flung it at her. She died hard. Her fictitious nature was of great assistance to her. It is far harder to kill a phantom than a reality.

One of my reasons for writing this essay is the persistence of a Mormon angel in the house. In my work at Brigham Young University, in conversations with my neighbors and friends in Mormon suburbia, in church and public meetings I hear too many women apologize for their statements of power as they acknowledge concern about women's issues and protest the current state of affairs. At the university I was frequently dismayed by how students recoiled at the very mention of feminism. Often I was accused in my student evaluations of being a feminist (although I was also accused of being a Democrat or even a socialist). Male and female students alike became defensive during discussions of historical feminism. It was as if they felt they had something to lose.

I hear too many apologies. At a recent professional meeting of the Mormon Historical Association in Lamoni, Iowa, one of my colleagues, an editor and writer, prefaced her remarks about women by saying, "Now I'm not a feminist, but I do believe women should be treated fairly." What does that mean? Of what was she afraid? Why does she want us to know she isn't a feminist? I recently appeared on a local Salt Lake City television program that discussed Mormonism and feminism; afterwards, numerous individuals wrote letters to the First Presidency of the Mormon church complaining about my continued employment at BYU because of my feminist views, describing me as brazen, dangerous, frumpy, a junior Betty Friedan, among other incendiary accusations. I was asked to answer these complaints, essentially to defend myself, a proposition I consider today entirely absurd. I am a feminist, and I do not need nor intend to apologize for it.

How did this happen? How did an atmosphere of suspicion and fear evolve to paint feminists as the enemy of traditional values? We feminists are the Reds of an earlier generation. Many believe we pose the most significant threat yet confronted in the twentieth century to the integrity of the LDS church and the patriarchal powerhold of the Mormon community.

In attempting to understand why there are so few Mormon feminists and why we are viewed with hostility, I will discuss three issues in the context of Mormon history: 1) The narrowing of women's political power within the community; 2) the idealization of the role of Mormon women; and 3) theological restraints to feminism within Mormonism.

I begin with an historical overview. During the nineteenth century the debate over female roles was called "The Woman Question." It was a grave preoccupation of families, churches, and politicians in much the same way as economic recession and nuclear weapons are today. Popular sensibility was dominated by an angry perplexity about why women might want to have spheres of influence outside the home—with growing numbers of women pointing out, the joys and cares of domesticity notwithstanding, there was no reason to suppose that housekeeping and intimate relationships could possibly satisfy every talent, ability, and inclination which half the human race might harbor.

In the midst of such controversy, Mormon women entered the twentieth century on the crest of a wave of institutional and personal power. They had joined with national feminists in the National Peace movement, the drive for female suffrage, and the national agenda for reform. The Mormon Relief Society, the Young Women's Mutual Improvement Association, and the children's Primary organization gave them opportunities for organizational power, leadership opportunities, and autonomy. Women were still performing blessings, anointings, and manifesting other spiritual gifts until the third decade of the twentieth century. In other words, they were still actively engaged in spiritual as well as social work.

During World War I the LDS church reorganized the women's Relief Society into units of the Red Cross for the war effort. This alignment with national agendas typified the engagement of Relief Society sisters in social causes during the first three decades of the twentieth century. The key player in this drama was Amy Brown Lyman.

Lyman first met with church president Joseph F. Smith in March 1918 to discuss the society's work with the Red Cross to benefit

Mormon servicemen and their families. She was at the time general secretary of the Relief Society. Lyman and a number of other women had already received professional training in the latest social work techniques, and President Smith himself was impressed. He commented: "If there was anything in the Church that needed improvement it was the charity work" because there was "much duplication and waste of effort and funds."[1] Smith offered to fund a social service department for the church and placed it at Relief Society headquarters, physically and organizationally under female leadership. This marriage of public and religious interests created the perfect vehicle for Lyman's creative energies.

Lyman first enrolled in sociology courses while her husband Richard attended the University of Chicago. There she became familiar with scientific approaches to societal problems, which she would later describe as having drawn a curtain from her mind.[2]

Under the Relief Society, the Church Social Services department worked closely with public agencies including the county charity department, the county hospital, the city and county courts, the county jail, the police department, the Salvation Army, the Traveler's Aid Society, the YWCA, and the Charity Organization Society.[3] This cooperative relationship with government agencies continued during the depression years and was facilitated by New Deal programs. The Federal Emergency Relief Administration required that federal funds be distributed through government agencies. This federalized the Relief Society Social Services Department for an eighteen-month period beginning in August 1933 while a state public welfare agency

---

1. Amy Brown Lyman, "Social Service Work in the Relief Society, 1917-1928," typescript, 4, Amy Brown Lyman Collection, Manuscripts Division, Harold B. Lee Library, Brigham Young University, Provo, Utah.

2. Amy Brown Lyman, "Interview at KSL," no date, typescript, 3, Amy Brown Lyman Collection, Lee Library; Amy Brown Lyman, *In Retrospect: Autobiography of Amy Brown Lyman* (Salt Lake City: General Board of Relief Society, 1945), 30, 114.

3. Amy Brown Lyman, "Social Service Work in the Relief Society, 1917-1928," typescript, 4-B, Amy Brown Lyman Collection, Lee Library, Brigham Young University.

was being created. Besides normal case work, Lyman's Relief Society staff provided food, clothing, and fuel orders from government stores.

These women were not stay-at-home mothers, staging teas and socials. They were feminists. They devoted their lives and energy to the feminist agenda. They were involved in social welfare, prenatal health, infant mortality projects such as the Relief Society milk stations, suffrage, moral education, and pacifism. In this historical context, Mormon women were feminists because they were involved in the issues of feminism.

Furthermore they were serious about their work. It defined them. And while it certainly did not preclude their obligations as mothers and wives they considered social activism a serious reason for their organizational existence. A sense of social responsibility and personal empowerment rings clear in the columns of the organization's publication—the *Relief Society Magazine*, Mar. 1939, 161-62. For instance, one column written by Clarissa Smith Williams and Amy Brown Lyman, "The Official Round Table," detailed Lyman's work in Colorado.[4] Amy Brown Lyman "has been spending a month in Denver studying social service methods in the headquarters of the Civic Service division there," it reads.

> The peace armistice has measurably halted our strenuous war activities . . . but the Relief Society workers will not cease their efforts and loyal labors until our Government gives the word that we are entirely released. . . . We received an appeal from the National Suffrage Association to join with them in memorializing President Wilson to add at least one woman to the Peace Commission, as women's and children's interests demand recognition at the hands of the men who are to settle the affairs of the world.

Isn't this extraordinary? The Mormon Relief Society joined in with one of the two most prominent women's organizations formed to promote the feminist agenda. These efforts in the full spectrum of social and moral progressive reform typified the work of the Relief

---

4. Clarissa Smith Williams and Amy Brown Lyman, "The Official Round Table," *Relief Society Magazine* 6 (Jan. 1919): 41-42.

Society during this interesting period of female empowerment. They were recognized for their work on a national and international scale. They were social activists, empowered by a sense of spirit, of self and corporate worth, and the institutional backing of the church.

In public forums these women addressed issues of national reform. Speakers at the 1919 Relief Society conference gave evidence of this emphasis. One woman, Cora Kasius, who, with Amy Brown Lyman, was one of the first Mormon women to receive professional social work training, spoke about the agenda for "transforming the unstable inefficient family to a stable efficient one."[5] The second speaker, Clarissa Smith Williams, suffragist Emmeline B. Wells's counselor and successor, urged the calling of "well-trained and well-educated" younger women as teachers because education was below the "standard desired for it." Other speakers addressed health, home nursing, juvenile delinquency, work with needy and dependent families, mental hygiene, and applied psychology. Equally interesting is the editorial written by Julia A. F. Lund, then general secretary-treasurer, defining the Relief Society's goals as "health, employment, social services, spiritual welfare, education in every form, better homes, [and] wiser parenthood."[6]

Toward the end of World War II, male leaders redefined the role of women in Mormon society and placed a new emphasis on raising families. In perhaps the single most important official move affecting the relationship of women to their church, on 29 July 1946 general Relief Society president Belle Spafford received a letter from Elder Joseph Fielding Smith of the LDS Quorum of the Twelve Apostles stating that it was no longer approved "for sisters to wash and anoint other sisters." Instead, women were to "send for the Elders . . . to come and administer to the sick and afflicted." Institutional sanction for women performing ordinances of healing was thus officially revoked.[7] Mormon women themselves had rethought their role

---

5. Amy Brown Lyman, "General Conference of the Relief Society," *Relief Society Magazine* 6 (Dec. 1919): 693.

6. Julia A. F. Lund, "Relief Society, A Significant Woman's Movement," *Relief Society Magazine* (Mar. 1939) 161-62.

7. Cited in D. Michael Quinn, "150 Years of Truth and Consequences

during the war. Women who had believed they could help save the world looked inward and focused on solving the problems of their own families instead.

Like the rest of the American nation recoiling from war, in 1949 the domestication of Mormon women was idealized even as their spiritual power eroded. The same phenomenon had occurred after the Revolutionary War with a call to "republican motherhood." In the rhetoric of those post-war decades, women played a key role. Men would fight the British and win the war, but it was women's responsibility to inculcate American values in their children's hearts and minds. Their role was to perpetuate and transmit the values, beliefs, and behavior that marked a republican nation.

By 1949 Mormon women, with their American female counterparts, joined the post-war celebration of domesticity, and increasingly the rhetoric of motherhood replaced the emphasis on social activism. The *Relief Society Magazine* became obsessed with the home and included an increased number of articles by men. Male voices acquired more authority and helped to define and articulate the Mormon female ideal. This ideological process continued to develop throughout the most passionate events of the 1960s women's movement and was by the early 1970s rigidified within church literature and practice.

During the LDS "correlation" movement of the 1970s the church pulled the auxiliaries of the church, including their publications and lesson materials, under one umbrella. The women of the Relief Society lost in 1971 their control over money and direct access to the LDS First Presidency. All LDS women automatically became members of the Relief Society, dues were no longer collected, and they were forbidden to have separate fundraising activities or budgets. Local wards no longer staged bazaars, bake sales, and other traditional activities that helped create and sustain female ward networks. The LDS church made considerable efforts to draw boundaries between traditional women and feminists. Increasingly the feminist was portrayed as the enemy of home, family, and traditional religious values.

---

about Mormon History," *Sunstone*, Feb. 1992, 14.

Nationally, the church's fight against the Equal Rights Amendment was essentially a war against feminism. On 13 December 1974
Barbara B. Smith, Relief Society general president, led the effort
taking a personal and public stance against the ERA in a speech
given at the LDS Institute adjacent to the University of Utah. While
acknowledging historical inequities to women and conceding the
impotency of legislative remedies, she insisted that "equal in life,
liberty, and the pursuit of happiness" was not the same thing as
"identical."[8] On 11 January 1975 an editorial in the *Church News*
criticized the ERA as "so broad that it is inadequate, inflexible, and
vague. . . . Men and women are different, made so by a Divine
Creator. Each has his or her role."[9]

In May 1978 the First Presidency officially launched the campaign
against ERA by issuing a statement opposing extension of the ratifi-
cation date, citing "profound veneration for the Constitution" and
"very deep and everlasting commitment to the preservation and
strengthening of the family."[10]

Anti-ERA activity stepped up in the late 1970s, including intervention in International Women's Year conferences and feminist
Sonia Johnson's 1979 excommunication. In February 1980 the
church published an anti-ERA booklet called: *The Church and the
Proposed Equal Rights Amendment: A Moral Issue.* It detailed among
other conclusions that the ERA would "endanger time-honored
moral values" by removing protective legislation, increasing access to
abortion, legalizing homosexual marriages, making women liable for
the draft, reducing a husband's legal requirement to support his wife
and children, eroding the power of the state, and possibly refusing
to recognize "reasonable distinctions between the sexes."

Victorian America was preoccupied with the role women played
as mothers and continued to romanticize it through the turn of the

---

8. Barbara Smith, oral interview with Jessie Embry, 1977, James B.
Moyle Oral History Program, archives, historical department, Church of
Jesus Christ of Latter-day Saints, Salt Lake City, Utah.

9. Lori Winder Stromberg, "LDS Position on the ERA: An Historical
View," *Exponent II* 6 (Winter 1980), 2:6-7.

10. Ibid., 7.

century. Mormon attitudes toward women and motherhood were not unique but paralleled those of the nation at large. The Victorian image provided a detailed model for motherhood which was adopted practically wholesale by Mormon culture and remained the primary image of motherhood during the next thirty or forty years. As was true of republican motherhood, what some scholars have called the cult of true womanhood included the idealization of mother's self-sacrifice, love, domesticity, and divine purity and gentleness. It is ironic that this all played out against a history of serious organizational work in feminism.

The sentimentalization of motherhood was increasingly perpetuated by the male hierarchy. One Mormon male speaker, Heber Iverson, in a 1923 radio address said: "the standards of motherhood during any given period of history are absolutely the controlling moral factors in the world at the time. The standards of civilization are fixed by woman. The quality of the manhood of every period is created by woman."[11] David O. McKay, second counselor in the First Presidency, called motherhood "the noblest office or calling in the world," "the greatest of all professions," and "the greatest potential influence either for good or ill in human life."[12]

Showing the importance of this body of ideas, the church mobilized powerful instruments to convince girls and women that motherhood was their primary role and obligation. Mormon leaders used an interesting variety of appeals. "The women who prefer society, entertainment, luxury, even a career, to motherhood, are not really intelligent," one leader noted. He further warned, "Divorce is a very much more frequent thing in families where a woman has economic independence and no children than under older fashioned conditions."[13] The accusation that women who were reluctant to bear

11. Heber C. Iverson, 5 Apr. 1908, *Seventy-eighth Annual Conference of the Church of Jesus Christ of Latter-day Saints* (Salt Lake City: Deseret News, 1908), 70-71.

12. David O. McKay, "Motherhood," address to the Sunday School of the Twenty-sixth Ward, Pioneer Stake, 14 May 1944, *Deseret News*, 20 May 1944.

13. Joseph J. Cannon, "The Glory of Motherhood: Its Spiritual,

children prevented the progress of unborn spirits was particularly potent.[14]

Even as church leaders were idealizing motherhood, Mormon women were following their Gentile sisters into employment out of the home. Alarmed, church leaders expressed disapproval of wage-earning mothers. When women began contributing to the war effort, the First Presidency said in 1942, "The mother who entrusts her child to the care of others, that she may do non-motherly work, whether for gold, for fame, or for civic service, should remember that a 'child left to himself bringeth his mother to shame.'"[15] A 1956 *Church News* editorial called "earning mothers" "one of the greatest threats we have to stable home life in America" and editorialized: "The Lord has said that he will hold parents responsible if they neglect their children, and working mothers and wives might well consider what he has said on the subject. There is no economic necessity today which will justify neglect of children."[16]

These ideas were emphasized visually in church publications. For example, drawings in the *Improvement Era* showed women working at the stoves in their homes, happily dusting tables, working in gardens in full skirted bliss, beaming smiles on their faces. They were not portrayed at desks in offices; rather than clients they had children and clearly enjoyed their domestic roles. These powerful images sent potent messages to women and girls that helped perpetuate the idealization of the female role, defined more narrowly after 1950 as mother.

Many women were particularly dissuaded from pursuing careers by LDS church president Ezra Taft Benson's pivotal address which characterized women's career objectives as selfish and degrading.

Physical, and Social Necessity as Conceived by Latter-day Saints," address, May 13, 1928, *Deseret News*, 19 May 1928.

14. J. Reuben Clark, Jr., "The Mission of Motherhood: What It Means in the Light of the Tenets Held Sacred by Latter-day Saints," address, 13 May 1928, *Deseret News*, 19 May 1928.

15. Message of the First Presidency, 3 Oct. 1942, 12.

16. "Should Mothers Go Out to Work?" editorial, *Church News*, 25 Aug. 1956, 16.

The most important work women can do is in the home, he reiterated, quoting a previous church president.[17] In March 1990 speaking at the University of Utah "Women in the Work Force Conference," Benson's counselor Gordon B. Hinckley added his voice: "It is my opinion that the very situation of an ever-increasing number of mothers out of the home and in the workplace is a root cause of many of the problems of delinquency, drugs, and gangs."[18]

This is a serious burden for mothers to carry on their shoulders. I have often wondered why fathers aren't similarly judged. Many women work for the same reasons as their husbands: the physical sustenance of their children. This blanket condemnation of what they do—their contributions—denigrates their efforts and devalues what they are.

Mormon leaders used to acknowledge women's equal burden; increasingly today the emphasis is on difference, not equality. For instance, one article in the *Relief Society Magazine* discussed Joseph F. Smith's "Vision of the Redemption of the Dead," which the magazine believed "confirms the noble standard of equality between the sexes which has always been a feature of the Church."[19] Today a number of inconsistent attitudes and policies separate men from women in the church.

Throughout their lives Mormon girls are given contradictory messages about their roles. They are told to be the best that they can be, but also to be supportive, submissive, obedient, and accepting. My daughter Katelyn wishes that official Mormon publications included more female imagery. "All the pictures of missionaries," she complained to me, "are men or boys." Young girls must be challenged by the church's policy of male priesthood ordination, wondering why they're not good enough to receive it themselves.

In 1979 University of Utah student Ann Kenney was set apart as

---

17. Ezra Taft Benson, *To the Mothers in Zion* (Salt Lake City: Church of Jesus Christ of Latter-day Saints, 1987).

18. "Journalist Ellerbee and President Hinckley Differ," *Sunstone*, 14 (Apr. 1990), 2:54-55.

19. "In Memoriam: Joseph F. Smith," *Relief Society Magazine* 6 (Jan. 1919): 5.

president of the University of Utah Second Stake Sunday School. The local stake leader who chose her explained that he had been "strongly impressed" to issue the call, which was approved by a church general authority. One month later, however, Kenney was released. She was told, "In the past there has been no policy set. The Quorum [of the Twelve] was divided on the issue, and the decision was left to the president [of the quorum]." The president was Ezra Taft Benson.[20]

The issue of leadership extends upwards. In the early church there were countless references to Mother in Heaven, glorious Mother Eve, and heroic women past and present.[21] Yet on 5 April 1991 President Hinckley warned church leaders "to be alert" to "small beginnings of apostasy" and cited prayers to Mother in Heaven as an example.[22] Belief in a mother in heaven figured prominently in the September 1993 disciplinary courts held for Mormon Women's Forum president Lynne Kanavel Whitesides.

Why the sustained attack against women? One reason is the growing number of working Mormon women, in spite of inequalities they experience in the workplace. Statistics gathered by the Utah Department of Employment Security reported that Utah is last in the nation in the number of women who perform top management jobs in state and local government (17.7 percent—the national average is less than one-third). In private business, 39 percent of executives and administrators are women, which is closer to the national trend. Between about 1950 and 1980 fully-employed women in Utah earned approximately sixty cents for every dollar a fully-employed man made.

More significant are increases in the number of working mothers. In 1980, 37 percent of Utah mothers with preschoolers were employed out of the home; in 1990, 57 percent of the same group were

---

20. "Church Tradition Now a Policy," *Sunstone* 10 (Feb. 1985), 2:32-33.

21. See the various essays in *Sisters in Spirit: Mormon Women in Historical and Cultural Perspective*, eds. Maureen Ursenbach Beecher and Lavina Fielding Anderson (Urbana: University of Illinois Press, 1987).

22. "Cornerstones of Responsibility," address delivered by President Gordon B. Hinckley at the Regional Representatives Seminar, Friday, 5 Apr. 1991; see also Nov. 1991 *Ensign*.

employed.[23] These figures do not include the huge number of Mormon women who work part time, which is even more typical, or women who essentially engage in sweat shop work in their homes. I know one woman who sews appliqued designs on twelve sweatshirts a day, proud that she isn't a working woman but able to stay home with her children. This is difficult, laborious work that requires enormous concentration. Even if she is in the house with her children I can't imagine that they are getting what they need from her. This admonition to mothers to stay at home confuses quality child care issues and fair labor condition standards, among other social issues that affect families.

National exposure to women's issues is unrelenting. We are continually bombarded with female imagery of empowerment. Can you imagine the impact of a whole generation of little Mormon girls growing up with the image of Hillary Clinton before them? Or Claire Huxtable? Or whomever? This is a generation who will grow to maturity with the image of Anita Hill as part of their female conscious-ness. How could it not make a difference?

Mormon women have organized and have reached a new level of sophistication in their discourse about feminism. I credit the Mor-mon Women's Forum and *Exponent II* for this accomplishment. While the forum's presentations have been significantly diverse and varied in quality, this important scene of feminist dialogue has continued to thrive despite numerous efforts to punish leaders for their participation, including the disfellowshipment of forum presi-dent Lynne Kanavel Whitesides and threats against Margaret Tos-cano and forum organizer Karen Crist.

The situation is bleak at best at BYU for feminist faculty and students. A recent study of BYU's female faculty shows that 13 percent of the total faculty are women; a handful are administrators; 3 percent full professors; 16 percent are associate professors; 23 percent assistant professors; 53 percent of instructors and adjunct professors are women. Until the 1960s BYU had a policy against

---

23. Nancy Hobbs, "Utah's Last in Placing Women in Top State, Local Positions," *Salt Lake Tribune*, 3 Dec. 1992, A-1, A-2.

hiring married women professors. Until the mid-1980s they had a policy against hiring mothers with school-aged children.

There have always been fine female instructors, professors, and employees of BYU who made an important contribution. And I do not in any way want to diminish the value of what they have given the university. But this new generation is important in different ways. We confronted feminism as young women. When we went to graduate school we were taught by feminist professors, we studied feminist methodologies, and we considered ourselves feminists without being threatened by what it seemed to represent.

There is now at BYU an activist group of feminists who are stirring things up like never before. They are inspiring a whole generation of young Mormon women to take on careers, to prepare themselves for the eventualities of life, and are exposing them to the great promise life holds for them, very definitely an expansive view. This is an irreversible process, no matter how many of us they fire or push out. We have made our imprint on that place. They will never forget us, nor us them, even though I have resigned from BYU. We helped to change things for young women not even born. This is a fight for all Mormon women and this time it played out on the tidy lawns and antiseptic classrooms of BYU. But it is well to remember that it isn't over yet. In part because so many of us have daughters, because we care about our female students, the difficult, perhaps horrible, work ahead takes on new poignancy and meaning.

The church's reaction against feminist expression is destructive. Children are juxtaposed against professional contributions. This illogical dichotomy presents feminists as the enemies of mothering, of the home. Who wouldn't be afraid of feminism when it is presented in this way?

In her book *Women Who Run With the Wolves*, Jungian psychologist Claudia Pinkola Estes discusses the importance of embracing Skeleton Woman, a dual-natured fertility figure that surfaces in certain Eskimo traditions. Skeleton Woman is a heap of bones after being punished by her father. She lives at the bottom of a lake until a fisherman, thinking he has made a big catch, snags her bones and reels her in. He is horrified at the sight of the skeleton rising from the lake and tries to escape. But her body is caught on the fishing line and no matter how hard he paddles she is still connected to the boat, and as he rows away she appears to be chasing him, rising again and again in the wake of the boat. When he realizes that he cannot get away, he stops and builds a fire. Though frightened and exhausted, he is finally overcome with compassion and proceeds to untangle the heap of bones that are twisted upon themselves. After covering her with a bear skin, he falls asleep before the fire. During the night, the Skeleton Woman acquires flesh. When the fisherman awakes he is no longer lying next to a skeleton, but the soft, rounded form of a woman. She releases him from his long loneliness, and provides him with companionship that will nourish them both for the rest of their days.

I believe that fear of Skeleton Woman, which so easily can represent the feminist, has been designed by a male hierarchy but perpetuated by faithful and obedient women. They are the ones who spend far too much time wrestling with her bones, trying to free themselves from the threat she seems to pose, a specter created for us by others. Too many women have been indoctrinated as girls to believe they cannot or should not or will not be powerful. And by the time they are women they are convinced. And they are afraid every time that Skeleton Woman, the face of feminism, shows itself before them. It is fear of the unknown, fear of failing at the most sacred institution in their charge, their families, that prevents many Mormon women from joining in the work.

This past year the BYU Women's Conference committee presented the name of Pulitzer Prize winning author Laurel Thatcher Ulrich as the keynote speaker to the school's board of trustees. Ironically, the two female members of the board were both out of town. The board rejected her name because of numerous early publications she produced for publications like *Dialogue* and *Exponent II*, a Mormon feminist publication she helped organize. This so incensed the female intellectual community that a group of women called for an alternate conference. And in April 1993 a small but courageous group of women chose to speak out and take a stand whatever the costs and organized Counterpoint Conference. After pressure was leveled against faculty in the BYU English department, seventeen professors chose to withdraw from the program, and only one student from BYU stayed on the program and participated. Most did not even attend. Consider the words of one professor, a feminist, as she expressed her reasons for withdrawing:

> After talking to several administrators and colleagues at BYU and giving the matter much thought, I have decided with profound regret, to withdraw from the conference. I am convinced that the concerns I feel deeply about in my department and in the University at large will be compromised if I speak at this time, but not because anything I would say would be divisive or in any way critical of the LDS Church. Due to the present political climate in Utah and the polarization within the Church membership and leadership, I don't believe my message will be fairly assessed. . . . This decision leaves me feeling quite hopeless; I see little possibility of ever having my own particular point-of-view heard. As a BYU faculty member, I do not believe women's very real issues are addressed adequately. I often feel overwhelmed by the pain that women students and colleagues express.[24]

It is impossible to have traveled through the fall of 1993 without a knowledge of the Mormon church's fear of feminism. The series of excommunications has been stimulated at least in part by the fear of powerful women, women empowered by ideas, and women willing to voice their criticism of church leaders. Certainly Apostle Boyd K. Packer's biting condemnation of feminists as one of the three most serious threats to the integrity of the church today—Mormon intellectuals and homosexuals were the other two—sends a potent message to Mormon women: "Stay home, be silenced, accept traditional ways of doing things, be good, be happy." But too many women believe the messages taught them as children, that they too, like their Mormon brothers are children of God, that they are of value, and that they must be the best that they can be. Anything less, and they fail in the most important commission they have been given.

If Mormon feminists represent the hideous face of Skeleton Woman rising again and again to haunt and confuse the leadership of this church, we must hope that leaders will eventually recognize in the guise of the Mormon feminist something of value, that acceptance

---

24. Copy in my possession.

of the fear we seem to create offers the hope of great power and strength that will benefit us all.

12.
Dancing Through the Doctrine: Observations on Religion and Feminism

Cecilia Konchar Farr

Lucretia Mott, a nineteenth-century Quaker minister and suffragist, delivered a speech at a Philadelphia women's rights convention in 1854 in which she discussed the day of Pentecost. She said:

> Then Peter stood forth—some one has said that Peter made a great mistake in quoting the prophet Joel—but he stated that "the time is come, this day is fulfilled the prophecy when it is said, I will pour out my spirit upon all flesh, your sons and your daughters shall prophesy," etc.—the language of the Bible is beautiful in its repetition—"upon my servants and my handmaidens I will pour out my spirit and they shall prophesy." Now can anything be clearer than that?[1]

Sarah Kimball, a nineteenth-century Mormon Relief Society leader and suffragist, held similar beliefs about the relationship between religion and suffrage, about the evidence of God's hand in the expansion of women's rights. She wrote that "the sure founda-

---

1. Miriam Schneir, ed., *Feminism: The Essential Historical Writings* (New York: Vintage, 1972), 102.

tions of the suffrage cause were deeply and permanently laid on the 17th of March, 1942," the day in LDS history when Joseph Smith "turned the key in the name of the Lord" to organize the Women's Relief Society.[2]

It is not unusual to find among early leaders of the cause of women's rights repeated and sincere references to religion. Sarah M. Grimke, for example, wrote that God created man *and woman* in his image: "God created us equal;—he created us free agents;—he is our Lawgiver, our King and our Judge, and to him alone is woman bound to be in subjection, and to him alone is she accountable for the use of those talents with which her Heavenly Father has entrusted her."[3] Sojourner Truth reminded her congregation that Jesus came "from God and a woman. Man had nothing to do with Him."[4] Elizabeth Cady Stanton, Susan B. Anthony, Fanny Fern, and of course our Mormon suffragists used religious doctrines as the foundation of feminism.

We have walked a long road since then, a road that has led us further and further away from religious discourse and Christian justification. Our reasons, like those of our liberal and humanist friends, have been good: we didn't want to limit or exclude. We didn't want to direct all feminists down a single philosophical path. We wanted to avoid the violence caused by binary thinking and metaphysical justifications. We've tread lightly, acknowledging but mostly avoiding sacred ground. Although academic feminists have revised history, philosophy, literature, and art while standing firmly within the narrow confines of patriarchal disciplines, our critiques of religion most often find us smelling the flowers to the side of the road. We don't often publicly state allegiance, even to the gentle god of the New Testament, though many of us admit to loving Shakespeare. Even though American feminism's mainstream is still made up of "liberal feminists" whose agenda remains reform rather than revolution, our discussions of religion are most often about women's

---

2. Jill Mulvey Derr, *Sarah M. Kimball* (Salt Lake City: Utah State Historical Society, 1976), 7.

3. Schneir, 37.

4. In Schneir, 95.

inherent (individual) spirituality or about the intractable patriarchal nature of the church—not about how to find women's place within mainstream religious movements. We work within patriarchal systems of education, economics and government, but we give up on religion. Why?

If there is a purpose for this essay, it is to call for two things: 1) a move on the part of American feminist organizations and theorists to reassert our ability to occupy the important ground of religious discourse and 2) a loyal feminist critique of religion on our way to a revolution in religious thinking, the Second Coming, if you will. We need to find out what is worth keeping in our traditional theology as we've done, for example, in philosophy. Many feminists no longer accept the Western humanist construct of a whole and unitary individual with inalienable rights, but we've taken off from that concept, empowered by deconstruction and revision, to explore new theories of subjectivity.

I see the return of religious rhetoric to feminist thinking as a way to overturn the binary of good and evil that is doing violence to our nation on issues such as abortion and child-care. Evoking religious morality on both sides blurs the distinctions between entrenched opposites. And it is an honest invocation, considering how many of us in the U.S. (liberal and conservative alike) connect our morality with an organized religion. I also see feminism as inclusionary: American feminism has embraced the American tradition of pluralism and done a much better job of encompassing diversity than most theoretical schools or political groups. We struggle constantly with the hows and whys, we make mistakes and fall into patriarchal and colonial patterns, but we never give up. As long as we as feminists maintain mutual respect for religion as we've done, I think fairly successfully, with sexual preference, this allowance of various religious discourses would do more to convince traditionally Catholic Chicana women, Jewish-American women, the religious Eastern European-American women I grew up with, African-American women whose ties are Christian or Muslim, or oppressed women of many ethnic groups who embrace liberation theology, that the movement belongs as much to them as to skeptical, middle-class, white-Anglo-Saxon-Protestant women.

As feminists, skilled in the discourse and practices of diversity, we'll have to apply our commitments across belief systems and resist the temptation of religious discourse to invoke the transcendent *as a proof*—as the ultimate end of discussion. We can't very well expect religion to do without a theory of transcendence—belief in God and a heaven beyond earth are, after all, what religion is about. But as one of my religious, postmodern students in a theory seminar said, "Keep your transcendence to yourself." Can religious feminists keep our religious proofs to communities of believers and approach others with gentle deference? I have seldom seen such deference in religious communities. Indeed, I understand that by inviting feminism to participate in religious discourse, I'm inviting feminism to work within a long history of violence, especially violence against women: witness the mass murder of "witches" in Europe and of "heathens" in Asia and the Middle East. This is more than a little problematic.

I have seen (and continue to see) such deference, such attention to different beliefs and cultures, within the feminist movement. Even so, in my study of feminisms I have yet to find a home for my conservative religious beliefs. I have found, instead, that religion is one area where mainstream feminist thinking has been clearly secular and often barely distinguishable from current mainstream liberalism. For example, we could easily substitute "feminism" for "the nation" in the following passage from Yale Law Professor Stephen L. Carter's book, *A Culture of Disbelief:* "It is both tragic and paradoxical that now, just as [feminism] is beginning to invite people into the public square for the different points of view that they have to offer, people whose contribution to [feminism's] diversity comes from their religious traditions are not valued unless their voices seem somehow esoteric."[5] Carter writes that despite the strong religious tradition in American social reform—from suffrage and abolition to Civil Rights and anti-war—where "the public rhetoric of religion . . . had been largely the property of liberalism," suddenly and immutably the realm of religion has been ceded to the conservative right, so that "by the time of the 1992 Republican Convention, one had the eerie sense that the right was asserting ownership in God." Other recent texts on religion and politics have also traced the move from "religious sentiments, beliefs, and organizations" being "at the heart of a large number of contemporary social movements" to the current perception that religion is only for hard-line conservatives.[6]

Mormon culture, especially in the American West, has participated in this broader cultural trend, successfully uniting religious doctrine with politically conservative dogma: in the 1992 presidential campaign of Bo Gritz; in various editorials in my local *Utah County Journal*; and most recently in a special issue on "the conservative backlash" in the BYU campus newspaper, the *Daily Universe*.[7] In a front-page editorial for that issue, BYU political science teacher Bud Scruggs defended God, family, and hearth as the exclusive domain of the conservative Republican. His defense echoes Hyrum Andrus's 1965 book on Mormonism and conservative politics, in which the author posits that "in order to meet the problems that currently confront them, Latter-day Saints are bound by that which they hold sacred, to support an intelligent, conservative position in social, economic and political philosophy."[8] Such rhetoric moves feminists, political activists, and even Democrats from the center of the church into the margins. And since there has not been an equally successful countering of this rhetoric, nationally or locally, there we have remained.

But in the margins, the words of Martin Luther King, social reformer, activist, and Baptist minister, reverberate in the speeches of Jesse Jackson and Mario Cuomo and in the writings of Toni Morrison and Madeleine L'Engle. King's dream was decidedly not a secular one, and his speech on "Conscience and the Vietnam War" reinforces that:

> For those who question "Aren't you a civil rights leader?"—and thereby mean to exclude me from the movement for peace—I answer by saying that I have worked too long and hard now against

6. Anson Shupe and Jeffrey K. Hadden, eds., *The Politics of Religion and Social Change* (New York: Paragon, 1988), viii.

7. *Daily Universe*, 19 Sept. 1993, 1.

8. Hyrum L. Andrus, *Liberalism, Conservatism and Mormonism* (Salt Lake City: Deseret Book Co., 1965), ix.

segregated public accommodations to end up segregating moral concerns. Justice is indivisible ... In 1957 when a group of us formed the [Southern Christian Leadership Conference], we chose as our motto: "To save the *soul* of America." Now it should be incandescently clear that no one who has any concern for the integrity and life of America today can ignore the present war.[9]

Perhaps in response to this impassioned rhetoric of activists of the 1960s and early 1970s, mainstream American politics continued more determinedly along its path of secularization. While the causes of the secularization of politics are complex and beyond the scope of this essay, some of the reasons most often cited include the privileged position science and empirical thinking have held since the Enlightenment and especially in the twentieth century; the "modernization" of the West, including technological advances, urbanization, and a growing mass media; and broad efforts toward public (i.e., secular) education for children from all racial, ethnic, and socio-economic groups. The persistence of religious groups in the face of these advances has surprised many social scientists. Recently in many countries, most notably in the Middle East and in Eastern Europe, religious resurgence has served as "an expression of cultural authenticity."[10]

Certainly in the United States we cannot deny that religion is our legacy, and it has returned to the political realm with a vengeance since the 1980s—but again only on the conservative right. Stephen Carter blames the left for yielding, for "shedding religious rhetoric like a useless second skin." But I believe he misses part of the picture. Religious feminists, and certainly Mormon feminists, might lay some of the blame for the loss of religious discourse in feminism, not only to our reluctance to use it, but also to a wresting away of this language by the conservative groups who have set up feminists—along with witches and lesbians—as enemies of God. For many people steeped

---

9. Martin Luther King, *The Trumpet of Conscience* (San Francisco: Harper and Row, 1967), 24.

10. Emile Sahliyeh, ed., *Religious Resurgence and Politics in the Contemporary World* (Albany NY: State University of New York Press, 1990), vii.

in conservative thinking, "femi-nazis" are effectively silenced before they attempt to speak. I have encountered such people at BYU who simply cannot hear a word I say, even when I'm teaching Hemingway or sharing my belief in Jesus Christ.

Let me take a moment here to locate myself. As I write, I am a professor at BYU, although I am being forced to leave the university in late 1994. I generally call myself a radical feminist, meaning that I imagine huge changes, not just reformative or cosmetic changes, are going to be necessary to alter women's oppressed situation in our world. I am generally more sympathetic to re-visioning and rethinking than I am to reform, because our oppressive ways of operating in this world are so firmly entrenched that painting over them will never be enough. We need to strip our institutions down to the bare structures, then see if they need rebuilding or renovation. We don't repair structures by sitting in the middle of them and imagining that they're fixed.

But if these structures are, in poet Audre Lorde's term, the father's house, have feminists explored many ways to approach them—with the father's tools? With our own? Or do we build our own houses across the street? Or do we reject the imperialist constructions that deface that Earth and go off to live in canyons and deserts? My position on religious conservatism and feminism is that, with apologies to Mary Daly, Sonia Johnson, and Carol P. Christ, whom I admire, feminists have been spending too much time in the desert. I say this perhaps because beginning at age six I was enmeshed in my mother's personal religious revival and conversion from Catholicism to Mormonism. Mormonism was then and continues to be my conduit into the universe, my access to personal spirituality, to healing faith, and to empowering theology. It pushes the limits of my intellect, reminding me that there are many ways to construct and perceive truths, many, many of them beyond my power of understanding. It gives me a way, as a feminist theorist, to approach believers of any theology tenderly and with respect.

Though I have studied feminist theory and have been a committed feminist for years, I am still brought up short when we assume, as a group, that our feminist faith is New Age, goddess-worship, or earth-centered. At the "Take Back the Night" march in Salt Lake City last May, I and a few of my friends were dismayed to find our political protest of violence against women coupled with candlelight chants about our bodies and our blood. I honor the organizers' commitment to their faith, but I balk at the assumption that it is the faith of all feminists.

Perhaps I am also writing in response to the question that I hear often from many of my (as we say in Mormonism) gentile friends, "Why do you stay in such a male-dominated religion?" I am often tempted to ask them, admittedly begging the question, which institutions they associate with are not dominated by men—banks, government, academies, factories, hospitals? I stay because Mormonism means something to me at the deepest levels of my being. That response informs this essay.

Let me also add this caveat: I am neither historian—Mormon or otherwise—social scientist, nor theologian. I am a feminist literary critic, with a penchant for cultural critique, and a Mormon woman, anxiously engaged in finding a way to integrate a late-twentieth-century postmodern feminist consciousness with a lifelong commitment to faith and active participation in the LDS church and a conviction that, for some feminists, the basic structure of Mormonism can and ought to remain. I emphasize some feminists because in this difficult time we must acknowledge the struggle many Mormons have with that structure. What I share with you, then, is perhaps more aptly titled "justification" than "observation."

Within my call for the return of religion to feminism and feminism to religion, I would like to suggest a broader discussion than we have heretofore had of Mormon feminism. I hesitate to do this, since my first response to our present embattled position is to close ranks, yet I think it is time we looked to the future armed with a clear praxis and an articulate agenda. I should probably remind you that this is most definitely a loyal critique—both of feminism and of Mormonism—because my elaboration may cause you to forget that. As my friend and I used to say self-righteously, "We're from the rock 'n roll generation. We haven't learned to waltz around the truth." It is my truth, of course, but I advance it with no less vigor because of it.

Recently some feminist thinkers, Gloria Steinem among them, have called for a return to consciousness-raising groups as a way of bringing feminism back to local relevance and back into the everyday lives of women. Feminist thinkers, mostly in academe, have turned our movement into a theory, they argue, to the detriment of the movement. This nostalgic place, where feminism was about the "liberation" of individual women, is, I think, where Mormon feminism has remained.

In the spring of 1993 I attended my first Mormon feminist retreat, called "Pilgrimage," with several graduate students and English teachers—all women in our twenties or early thirties—who had met together once a week for nearly a year to study feminist theory. A combination consciousness-raising/support/study group, we had spent part of winter semester studying Mormon feminism. We read Sonja Johnson's *From Housewife to Heretic*, essays from *Sisters in Spirit*, and Maxine Hanks's collection, *Women and Authority*.[11] As we talked our way through these texts, we began to outline a Mormon feminism from our roots in feminist theory and cultural criticism, a feminism based only partly on our own experiences. This feminism, we decided, was not so much a reaction to disillusionment or mistreatment as it was an enactment of our theory and our theology.

At "Pilgrimage" our own thinking was set against the backdrop of the longstanding tradition of Mormon feminism which surrounded us there. We spent our days pointing out to each other known LDS feminists we had read—there're Linda King Newell in the sauna, Lavina Fielding Anderson by the fireplace, Margaret Toscano at the book display—and our nights sorting through our experience. Amid a group of women we admire and respect, here is what we saw at "Pilgrimage": a feminism based on individual liberation, where meetings consisted mainly of entertainment, affirmation, and sharing stories of awakenings and abuses; a homogeneous feminism that seemed, for the most part, comfortable in its familiar surroundings; an insular feminism that based its desires for change almost solely on getting male leaders to understand women in the church; a non-theoretical feminism, whose major premise was that women should no longer be silent; an apolitical feminism that, at the time, resisted a

---

11. Sonia Johnson, *From Housewife to Heretic* (Albuquerque, NM: Wildfire, 1989); Maxine Hanks, ed., *Women and Authority: Re-emerging Mormon Feminism* (Salt Lake City: Signature Books, 1993).

pull by some of its members into an activist campaign to wear white ribbons on their lapels.

It was, in short, a feminism we were not wholly comfortable with, a feminism that highlighted all of the imperfections of our smaller group—homogeneity, middle-class consciousness, insularity. It was also different from the Mormon feminism we had been developing hopefully together. Let me explain. One member of our group worked on the rape crisis hotline in Provo. She talked to rape victims, sometimes several a week, took them to the hospital and the police station. She insisted that we always keep broad social and cultural change on our agenda. Another woman studies Hispanic literature. She never let us forget that white women are not the center of the world—that we aren't even a majority of women in many parts of America. She inspired us to read Gloria Anzaldua together. Another had just finished teaching for a year in intercity schools in Boston and had, she told us, altered her approach to life at a very basic level to accommodate what she learned there. We made each other food, we threw showers and going-away parties, watched each other's children. We confided and theorized and negotiated. And we demonstrated, organized, and gave political speeches.

In short, though our discussions were local and personal, they were also theoretical and global, always with immense political and cultural pretensions. We saw how religious institutions resist change and close the doors to revolution; we were determined not so much to change the church as to change the world. Mormonism opens a skylight to revelation, and therein lies hope for changing the church—and we pray for it. But in the meantime there's a lot to be done, and we feminists must be about our Father's business, if you'll excuse my rallying you around a patriarchal metaphor. We need to be much more anxiously engaged beyond the boundaries of our small communities and our individual souls.

Let me acknowledge that many Mormon feminists see revolution and revelation as much more closely related than I do, and they courageously stake their integrity on it. To them I say, let the conversation begin. Because we are well-suited to initiate a discussion of religion and women's issues; we have a history of courageous feminists and a common bond that crosses cultures and ideologies.

It is a worldwide church, and many of us are lucky enough to serve in wards that reflect this.

In conclusion, I must insist that if you are committed to Christianity, you are committed to social change, to feeding the hungry, clothing the naked, mourning with those who mourn. You are bound to be humble in your assertions, reluctant to exercise authority, eager to serve others, and loving to those who believe differently. I say, with all due respect for difference, that I, as a Latter-day Saint, am bound by that which I hold sacred to support an intelligent, radical feminist position in social, economic, political, and religious philosophy.

Epilogue:
The Indispensable
Opposition (1939)

Walter Lippmann

[I]

Were they pressed hard enough, most men would probably confess that political freedom—that is to say, the right to speak freely and to act in opposition—is a noble ideal rather than a practical necessity. As the case for freedom is generally put today, the argument lends itself to this feeling. It is made to appear that, whereas each man claims his freedom as a matter of right, the freedom he accords to other men is a matter of toleration. Thus, the defense of freedom of opinion tends to rest not on its substantial, beneficial, and indispensable consequences, but on a somewhat eccentric, a rather vaguely benevolent, attachment to an abstraction.

It is all very well to say with Voltaire, "I wholly disapprove of what you say, but will defend to the death your right to say it," but as a matter of fact most men will not defend to the death the rights of other men; if they disapprove sufficiently what other men say, they will somehow suppress those men if they can.

So, if this is the best that can be said for liberty of opinion, that a man must tolerate his opponents because everyone has a "right" to say what he pleases, then we shall find that liberty of opinion is a luxury, safe only in pleasant times when men can be tolerant because they are not deeply and vitally concerned.

Yet actually, as a matter of historic fact, there is a much stronger foundation for the great constitutional right of freedom of speech, and as a matter of practical human experience there is a much more compelling reason for cultivating the habits of free men. We take, it seems to me, a naively self-righteous view when we argue as if the right of our opponents to speak were something that we protect because we are magnanimous, noble, and unselfish. The compelling reason why, if liberty of opinion did not exist, we should have to invent it, why it will eventually have to be restored in all civilized countries where it is now suppressed, is that we must protect the right of our opponents to speak because we must hear what they have to say.

We miss the whole point when we imagine that we tolerate the freedom of our political opponents as we tolerate a howling baby next door, as we put up with the blasts from our neighbor's radio because we are too peaceable to heave a brick through the window. If this were all there is to freedom of opinion, that we are too good-natured or too timid to do anything about our opponents and our critics except to let them talk, it would be difficult to say whether we are tolerant because we are magnanimous or because we are lazy, because we have strong principles or because we lack serious convictions, whether we have the hospitality of an inquiring mind or the indifference of an empty mind. And so, if we truly wish to understand why freedom is necessary in a civilized society, we must begin by realizing that, because freedom of discussion improves our own opinions, the liberties of other men are our own vital necessity.

We are much closer to the essence of the matter, not when we quote Voltaire, but when we go to the doctor and pay him to ask us the most embarrassing questions and to prescribe the most disagreeable diet. When we pay the doctor to exercise complete freedom of speech about the cause and cure of our stomachache, we do not look upon ourselves as tolerant and magnanimous, and worthy to be admired by ourselves. We have enough common sense to know that if we threaten to put the doctor in jail because we do not like the diagnosis and the prescription it will be unpleasant for the doctor, to be sure, but equally unpleasant for our own stomachache. That is why even the most ferocious dictator would rather be treated by a doctor who was free to think and speak the truth than by his own Minister of Propaganda. For there is a point, the point at which things really matter, where the freedom of others is no longer a question of their right but of our need.

The point at which we recognize this need is much higher in some men than in others. The totalitarian rulers think they do not need the freedom of an opposition: they exile, imprison, or shoot their opponents. We have concluded on the basis of practical experience, which goes back to the Magna Carta and beyond, that we need the opposition. We pay the opposition salaries out of the public treasury.

Insofar as the usual apology for freedom of speech ignores this experience, it becomes abstract and eccentric rather than concrete and human. The emphasis is generally put on the right to speak, as if all that mattered were that the doctor should be free to go to into the park and explain to the vacant air why I have a stomachache. Surely that is a miserable caricature of the great civic right which men have bled and died for. What really matters is that the doctor should tell me what ails me, that I should listen to him; that if I do not like what he says I should be free to call in another doctor; and that then the first doctor should have to listen to the second doctor; and that out of all the speaking and listening, the give-and-take of opinions, the truth should be arrived at.

This is the creative principle of freedom of speech, not that it is a system for the tolerating of error, but that it is a system for finding the truth. It may not produce the truth, or the whole truth all the time, or often, or in some cases ever. But if the truth can be found, there is no other system which will normally and habitually find so much truth. Until we have thoroughly understood this principle, we shall not know why we must value our liberty, or how we can protect and develop it.

[II]

Let us apply this principle to the system of public speech in a totalitarian state. We may, without any serious falsification, picture a condition of affairs in which the mass of the people are being addressed through one broadcasting system by one man and his chosen subordinates. The orators speak. The audience listens but cannot and dare not speak back. It is a system of one-way communication; the opinions of the rulers are broadcast outwardly to the mass of the people. But nothing comes back to the rulers from the people except the cheers; nothing returns in the way of knowledge of forgotten facts, hidden feelings, neglected truths, and practical suggestions.

But even a dictator cannot govern by his own one-way inspiration alone. In practice, therefore, the totalitarian rulers get back the reports of the secret police and of their party henchmen down among the crowd. If these reports are competent, the rulers may manage to remain in touch with public sentiment. Yet that is not enough to know what the audience feels. The rulers have also to make great decisions that have enormous consequences, and here their system provides virtually no help from the give-and-take of opinion in the nation. So they must either rely on their own intuition, which cannot be permanently and continually inspired, or, if they are intelligent despots, encourage their trusted advisers and their technicians to speak and debate freely in their presence.

On the walls of the houses of Italian peasants one may see inscribed in large letters the legend, "Mussolini is always right." But if that legend is taken seriously by Italian ambassadors, by the Italian General Staff, and by the Ministry of Finance, then all one can say is heaven help Mussolini, heaven help Italy, and the new Emperor of Ethiopia.

For at some point, even in a totalitarian state, it is indispensable that there should exist the freedom of opinion which causes opposing opinions to be debated. As time goes on, that is less and less easy under a despotism; critical discussion disappears as the internal opposition is liquidated in favor of men who think and feel alike. That is why the early successes of despots, of Napoleon I and of Napoleon III, have usually been followed by an irreparable mistake. For in listening only to his yes-men—the others being in exile or in concentration camps, or terrified—the despot shuts himself off from the truth that no man can dispense with.

We know all this well enough when we contemplate the dictatorships. But when we try to picture our own system, by way of contrast, what picture do we have in our minds? It is, is it not, that anyone may stand up on his own soapbox and say anything he please, like the individuals in Kipling's poem who sit each in his separate star and draw the Thing as they see it for the God of Things as they are. Kipling, perhaps, could do this, since he was a poet. But the ordinary mortal isolated on his separate star will have an hallucination, and a citizenry declaiming from separate soapboxes will poison the air with hot and nonsensical confusion.

If the democratic alternative to the totalitarian one-way broadcasts is a row of separate soapboxes, then I submit that the alternative is unworkable, is unreasonable, and is humanly unattractive. It is above all a false alternative. It is not true that liberty has developed among civilized men when anyone is free to set up a soapbox, is free to hire a hall where he may expound his opinions to those who are willing to listen. On the contrary, freedom of speech is established to achieve its essential purpose only when different opinions are expounded in the same hall to the same audience.

For, while the right to talk may be the beginning of freedom, the necessity of listening is what makes the right important. Even in Russia and Germany [in 1939] a man may still stand in an open field and speak his mind. What matters is not the utterance of opinions. What matters is the confrontation of opinions in debate. No man can care profoundly that every fool should say what he likes. Nothing has been accomplished if the wisest man proclaims his wisdom in the middle of the Sahara Desert. This is the shadow. We have the substance of liberty when the fool is compelled to listen to the wise man and learn; when the wise man is compelled to take account of the fool, and to instruct him; when the wise man can increase his wisdom by hearing the judgment of his peers.

That is why civilized men must cherish liberty—as a means of promoting the discovery of truth. So we must not fix our whole attention on the right of anyone to hire his own hall, to rent his own broadcasting stations, to distribute his own pamphlets. These rights are incidental; and though they must be preserved, they can be preserved only by regarding them as incidental, as auxiliary to the substance of liberty that must be cherished and cultivated.

Freedom of speech is best conceived, therefore, by having in mind the picture of a place like the American Congress, an assembly where opposing views are represented, where ideas are not merely uttered but debated, or the British Parliament, where men who are free to speak are also compelled to answer. We may picture the true condition of freedom as existing in a place like a court of law, where witnesses testify and are cross-examined, where the lawyer argues against the opposing lawyer before the same judge and in the presence of one jury. We may picture freedom as existing in a forum where the speaker must respond to questions; in a gathering of scientists where the data, the hypothesis, and the conclusion are submitted to men competent to judge them; in a reputable newspaper which not only will publish the opinions of those who disagree but will reexamine its own opinion in the light of what they say.

Thus the essence of freedom of opinion is not in mere toleration as such, but in the debate which toleration provides: it is not in the venting of opinion, but in the confrontation of opinion. That this is the practical substance can readily be understood when we remember how differently we feel and act about the censorship and regulation of opinion purveyed by different media of communication. We find then that, in so far as the medium makes difficult the confrontation of opinion in debate, we are driving towards censorship and regulation.

There is, for example, the whispering campaign, the circulation of anonymous rumors by men who cannot be compelled to prove what they say. They put the utmost strain on our tolerance, and there are few who do not rejoice when the anonymous slanderer is caught, exposed, and punished. At a higher level there is the moving picture, a most powerful medium for conveying ideas, but a medium which does not permit debate. A moving picture cannot be answered effectively by another moving picture; in all free countries there is some censorship of the movies, and there would be more if the producers did not recognize their limitations by avoiding political controversy. There is then the radio. Here debate is difficult; it is not easy to make sure that the speaker is being answered in the presence of the same audience. Inevitably, there is some regulation of the radio.

When we reach the newspaper press, the opportunity for debate is so considerable that discontent cannot grow to the point where under normal conditions there is any disposition to regulate the press. But when newspapers abuse their power by injuring people who have no means of replying, a disposition to regulate the press appears. When we arrive at Congress we find that, because the membership of the House is so large, full debate is impracticable. So there are restrictive rules. On the other hand, in the Senate, where the conditions of full debate exist, there is almost absolute freedom of speech.

This shows us that the preservation and development of freedom of opinion are not only a matter of adhering to abstract legal rights, but also, and very urgently, a matter of organizing and arranging sufficient debate. Once we have a firm hold on the central principle, there are many practical conclusions to be drawn. We then realize that the defense of freedom of opinion consists primarily in perfecting the opportunity for an adequate give-and-take of opinion; it consists also in regulating the freedom of those revolutionists who cannot or will not permit or maintain debate when it does not suit their purposes.

We must insist that free oratory is only the beginning of free speech; it is not the end, but a means to an end. The end is to find the truth. The practical justification of civil liberty is not that self-expression is one of the rights of man. It is that the examination of opinion is one of the necessities of man. For, experience tells us that it is only when freedom of opinion becomes the compulsion to debate that the seed which our fathers planted has produced its fruit. When that is understood, freedom will be cherished not because it is a vent for our opinions but because it is the surest method of correcting them.

The unexamined life, said Socrates, is unfit to be lived by man. This is the virtue of liberty, and the ground on which we may best justify our belief in it, that it tolerates error in order to serve the truth. When men are brought face to face with their opponents, forced to listen and learn and mend their ideas, they cease to be children and savages and begin to live like civilized men. Then only is freedom a reality, when men may voice their opinions because they must examine their opinions.

[III]

The only reason for dwelling on all this is that if we are to preserve democracy we must understand its principle. And the principle which distinguishes it from all other forms of government is that in a democracy the opposition not only is tolerated as constitutional but must be maintained because it is in fact indispensable.

The democratic system cannot be operated without effective opposition. For, in making the great experiment of governing people by consent rather than by coercion, it is not sufficient that the party in power should have a majority. That means that it must listen to the minority and be moved by the criticisms of the minority. That means that its measure must take account of the minority's objections, and that in administering measures it must remember that the minority may become the majority.

The opposition is indispensable. A good statesman, like any other sensible human being, always learns more from his opponents than from his fervent supporters. For his supporters will push him to disaster unless his opponents show him where the dangers are. So if he is wise he will often pray to be delivered from his friends, because they will ruin him. But, though it hurts, he ought also to pray never to be left without opponents; for they keep him on the path of reason and good sense.

The national unity of a free people depends upon a sufficiently even balance of political power to make it impracticable for the administration to be arbitrary and for the opposition to be revolutionary and irreconcilable. Where that balance no longer exists, democracy perishes. For unless all the citizens of a state are forced by circumstances to compromise, unless they feel that they can affect policy but that no one can wholly dominate it, unless by habit and necessity they have to give and take, freedom cannot be maintained.

Contributors

Robert Alley is professor of humanities at the University of Richmond, Virginia. His essay is adapted from a transcript of the address he delivered at the Mormon/Humanist Dialogue.

Lavina Fielding Anderson, proprietor of Editing, Inc., is a former associate editor of *The Ensign* and editor of the *Journal of Mormon History*.

Gary James Bergera is co-author (with Ron Priddis) of *Brigham Young University: A House of Faith* (Salt Lake City: Signature Books, 1985). His essay is adapted from a panel discussion on Academic Freedom at Brigham Young University, sponsored by the B. H. Roberts Society, held at the University of Utah on 16 September 1993.

Martha Sonntag Bradley is a former professor of history at Brigham Young University, associate professor of history at the University of Utah, and co-editor of *Dialogue: A Journal of Mormon Thought*.

Frederick S. Buchannan is professor of education at the University of Utah.

Bonnie Bullough is professor emeritus of nursing, State University of New York at Buffalo.

Vern L. Bullough is distinguished professor emeritus at State University of New York at Buffalo.

Cecilia Konchar Farr is professor of English at Brigham Young University.

Paul Kurtz is emeritus professor of philosophy at State University of New York at Buffalo and editor of *Free Inquiry* magazine.

Gerald Larue is professor emeritus of archaeology and biblical studies at the University of Southern California.

Walter Lippmann was an award-winning journalist and author who commented for many years on national and international affairs.

L. Jackson Newell is professor of educational administration at the University of Utah.

F. Ross Peterson is professor of history at Utah State University at Logan.

Allen Dale Roberts, architect in Salt Lake City, is co-editor of *Dialogue: A Journal of Mormon Thought*.